COURAGE

COURAGE
Jesus and the Call to Brave Faith

Courage
978-1-7910-1524-4
978-1-7910-1525-1 eBook

Courage: DVD
978-1-7910-1528-2

Courage: Leader Guide
978-1-7910-1526-8
978-1-7910-1527-5 eBook

ALSO BY TOM BERLIN

6 Decisions That Will Change Your Life

6 Things We Should Know About God

6 Ways We Encounter God

Bearing Fruit

Defying Gravity

The Generous Church

High Yield

Overflow

Reckless Love

Restored

TOM BERLIN

COURAGE

JESUS AND THE CALL TO
BRAVE FAITH

Abingdon Press / Nashville

COURAGE
Jesus and the Call to Brave Faith

Library of Congress Control Number: 2020950676
978-1-7910-1524-4

21 22 23 24 25 26 27 28 29 30—10 9 8 7 6 5 4 3 2 1
MANUFACTURED IN THE UNITED STATES OF AMERICA

To Bishop John Yambasu,
courageous leader and my dear friend.
Your life was defined by the joy and fortitude
that arises from a deep faith in Jesus Christ.

CONTENTS

INTRODUCTION

There is a Post-it note on my computer screen. I wrote it when Floris United Methodist Church, where I serve as lead pastor, was going through a time of self-definition. We were holding meetings to discuss the kind of church we wanted to be. Important issues were being discussed. I decided that I needed to make a list of what I owed the people of the congregation as their pastor. I wrote four words on that yellow slip of paper that remains there today:

Courage
Clarity
Candor
Encouragement

I realize now that I was starting a list of the elements of courage, beginning with those that I most needed to keep in front of me at that time. These words remind me of virtues I need to demonstrate. This was work that I needed to do at a time that was only made even more unusual when the global COVID-19 pandemic dramatically changed life in March 2020.

History reveals that courage is always needed in every time and in every place. The Christian life is the same. Courage is necessary for Christians to fulfill the mandates of their faith and live in ways consistent to the high calling of the gospel of Jesus Christ. Problems are numerous, opinions are many, and it is tempting to keep your head down and even disengage from relationships, institutions, problem-solving, and plans for the future.

Some other items have gathered on my desk with that list. There are a button, a metal figurine, a plaque, and a cross made by a child, along with others. You will see these in the chapters ahead. I realized recently that there was a reason that while other things on my desk come and go, these have remained for months and years. The common element of these items was that each reminded me of some aspect of courage.

I started thinking about courage when I was a high school senior. I had to write a major paper on one topic in *The Great Books of the Western World*. Ambitiously, I set out with this title: *The Formation and Training of the Courageous Man*. I was seventeen. I was neither courageous nor a man, but I had great aspirations.

That assignment became a major lens through which I observed the world around me in the years that followed. The most courageous person I know? Jesus. Reading the Gospels, one can see this quality emerge in diverse settings with all sorts of people. Jesus touches the untouchable. He stops to attend to people whose association would damage his reputation. He confronts power. He calls in sinners and calls out hypocritical religious leaders. He says hard things to his friends and family alike. He undertakes impossible tasks. Jesus calms storms while pitching about in a small boat. He faces accusers who bring suffering and death when it would be so much easier to get up and run. If you want to know about courage, you have to get to know

Jesus. Courage is an essential part of living well and it is an absolute requirement if one is going to follow Jesus in any meaningful sort of way, especially in times of hardship.

Courage is referenced in the Bible nearly one hundred times. Many of those times it is written as a command, to "take courage." This leads us to consider how we are to do that so readily. If the Bible would say, "Be afraid. Carry a lot of anxiety. Allow fear to keep you from doing important things in life," many of us would think, "Got it. I am living those words every single day."

"Take courage" is a bit harder. Where are we to find courage? Is there a courage well somewhere from which we draw? Is there a treasure map that will show us where to find a chest full of bravery? Is it like a pocketful of miracles or a shower of love, something readily available if only we had eyes to see? It seems unlikely.

Jesus is only known to have said the word *courage* one time in the Gospels. He is warning the disciples of his impending death. He tells them of the sorrow they will experience. He tries to answer their confused questions. He warns that they will all be scattered. Jesus says that they will abandon him and leave him to face his circumstances alone. Then he says,

> "I have said this to you, so that in me you may have peace. In the world you face persecution. But take courage; I have conquered the world!"
>
> (John 16:33)

Jesus wants his followers to understand that their courage is rooted in what he has already done. His words echo the words Moses offered the children of Israel before his death and their movement into the Promised Land in Deuteronomy 31. Moses reminded them that he was

120 years old. It was way past time for retirement. Joshua would now lead them. When you read the chapter, you can almost hear the sound of relief in his voice. When I was younger, I always thought Moses spoke his words as a final exhortation. I heard his words offered like a football coach's pep talk at halftime when the game hung in the balance. But I am less young now. I am young in a more mature sort of way. Now I hear Moses speaking like a father who is saying goodbye to his almost adult children as they depart for their first big trip without him. "Did you check the air pressure on the tires like I asked? Do you have a full tank of gas?" Now imagine Moses, in this same tone of voice, saying,

> "Be strong and courageous. Do not be afraid
> or terrified because of them, for the LORD your
> God goes with you; he will never leave you nor
> forsake you."
>
> (Deuteronomy 31:6 NIV)

It is less of a speech, and more of a blessing. Moses wants us to know that courage is present when we remember that God goes with us. Moses is confident that God will neither jilt them nor desert them. He's 120 years old. There is not much Moses hasn't seen, especially in the last forty years. Frankly, he is kind of ready for the children of Israel to give him a little peace and quiet. He'd like to have a little "me time" before he dies. I imagine Moses is not worried as they file past him, waving goodbye. He has come to realize that they do not need him to go with them. They need the Lord to go with them. Better yet, they need to go with the Lord. When you go with the Lord, you don't have to worry about fear and anxiety. Courage is walking right there beside you. The Lord has already overcome the world.

As a pastor, I have seen hundreds of people exhibit all sorts of courage: physical, social, moral, intellectual, and spiritual. I have seen them care for their families after a spouse died, stick with a child in crisis, go to war, work for peace, set relational boundaries, start a business, be the first in a family to graduate college, and much more. Watching them, I have tried to understand the nature of courage, where it most matters, and the qualities that are shared by people whose actions, words, and convictions are courageous. The people I admire and appreciate the most are those who exhibited courage in critical moments. They found their voice. They rose to the occasion. They took a stand. They did not give up. Their love did not fail. Here's a secret about my motivation: I learned from them because I wanted to be courageous myself.

Jesus calls us to a brave faith. In this book, we will look at the composition of what we call courage. Jesus will be our guide and our focus. In chapter 1, we look at the clarity required to evoke courage in our lives. Chapter 2 opens us to how the experience of conviction fuels courage and enables us to sustain it over time. A key area where courage is required is in important conversations. Speaking up is never easy, whether in our personal lives or the community in which we live. Candor, the ability to be vulnerable and open, is the focus of chapter 3. Chapter 4 considers the way hope sustains courage over the long run, even when circumstances do not go our way. Fortitude is the theme of chapter 5. I have seen people do bold things based on fortitude and a few words of commitment uttered decades in their past. Finally, love is the focus of chapter 6. We consider the love of Christ and the courage we see uniquely on display in the last week of Jesus's life.

I am not an expert on courage, but like you, I have had to be a practitioner. I write this book as a journey of learning. I wanted to understand the component parts of courage, how it is maintained, and how faith in Jesus Christ creates and informs a courageous life. I write as one seeking answers, because I believe that the person who leads the group is often the person who learns the most. If you want to live a courageous life, if you need to discover courage, or renew it in your life, I hope you will take this journey with me.

Chapter 1

THE CLARITY OF COURAGE

When they had come together, they asked Jesus, "Lord, is this the time when you will restore the kingdom to Israel?" He replied, "It is not for you to know the times or periods that the Father has set by his own authority. But you will receive power when the Holy Spirit has come upon you; and you will be my witnesses in Jerusalem, in all Judea and Samaria, and to the ends of the earth."

(Acts 1:6-8)

Last words are often clear words. Jesus is clear because he knows that the mission he describes, the mission that will define the rest of the disciples' lives, will require great courage. After leading them for three years, he spent forty days with them after his resurrection. Jesus the teacher is now Christ the Lord. No one can doubt that now. He is about to ascend into heaven. He is way past putting things in question form to those who have worshiped him and call themselves his disciples. He does not say, "I was kind of wondering if you all might be able to be my witnesses? I know how busy you all are but it would be helpful, and if it's not too much trouble, for you to go all the way to the ends of the earth." Christ is clear. He says, "You will be my witnesses." He tells them where to start, and where they can feel free to stop. This is a monumental task. They are to travel in places near and familiar, and to territories and countries they never knew existed, to share his teaching, his way of life, and the invitation to Christian discipleship. Jesus knows that they will be challenged. They will be rejected, persecuted, and imprisoned. This is a lot to ask from a group of people, the majority of whom abandoned him before his arrest only forty days ago. Clarity is everything in such moments.

RAISING THE MORAL TEMPERATURE

Just as tropical storms traveling across the ocean are powered by the rising of warm, moist air from the ocean, so courage gains strength when a person becomes clear about what it is God is asking him or her to accomplish. The warmer the air at the time of a hurricane, the more water vapor it can hold. Conversely, falling temperatures in the air or water will cause the storm to lose energy and dissipate. They weaken its ability to form into a hurricane. Courage begins to form in us when we experience the heat of clarity that arises when we see a circumstance we know we can help change or feel compassion for a person we know we can help. It may be a mission that attracts us, a cause we are to undertake, or a person or group of people we are to assist. When we lack this clarity, courage has no way to develop, as questions about whether we should be involved will emerge. Confusion over the outcomes we seek and questions about whether something is important enough to gain our attention are like cold ocean waters that throw the brakes on a tropical storm.

Years ago I asked my friend Mark, also a pastor, to join me in a mission to help war-impacted children in Sierra Leone, Africa, through the Child Rescue Centre. The conversation went something like this:

Me: "You have to get involved in this. You care about children and the needs there are great. It is a great opportunity for you and your church."

Mark: "I am in a growing church and I am busy all the time. We just completed a building campaign. We can't take on one more thing. This is great, and I will support you with my prayers. Maybe we can take a special offering sometime to help."

Me: "It will not just serve the children there. Your involvement will be life-changing for you!"

Mark: "I just don't think this is a good point in my life to do that. Maybe down the road I'll get involved."

Rather than continue to ask him to support the ministry, I asked him to give me thirteen days to go with me and see it for himself. I mentioned that it was not an easy journey, and he would have to bring his "lowest maintenance self." Mark said he was not sure he had one of those. I was afraid I may have scared him off, but he showed up on the day of departure anyway. It was a long trip. There were planes, cars, and a very old helicopter. The final leg included a six-hour van ride. Mark and I sat in the back seat over the hole in the floorboard beneath our feet. The dust from the dirt road, combined with car exhaust, made breathing difficult. We tied bandannas in front of our faces to filter the dust. From a comfort perspective, it was easily the worst road trip either of us had ever taken. While he took it all in with great humor, I was sure I was losing him fast.

Over the next few days we spent time talking, playing, and reading with the children at the Child Rescue Centre. We met with our partners there and learned about their hopes for the future and their desire to bless more children through foster care and adoption services. They showed us the tremendous need to help children find education, not only due to the recent civil war, but the ongoing problem of child labor that left people uneducated and unequipped to advance in adult life.

Mark came to me one evening and said, "Well, this is exactly what I thought would happen. It's the reason I didn't want to come. Now that I have met the children, I really feel a sense of love and concern for them. I understand the needs and the opportunities here. And now I am going to have to go back and do all the things I knew would be so hard to do! And you are to blame for this! So thanks. I think."

When Mark returned to his church, he had clarity. The difficulty of the trip was now a story of adventure rather than discomfort. He told his congregation about his trip and asked them to get involved. Many took the trip to Bo, Sierra Leone, themselves. They raised funds and took leadership roles in our partnership. Because of their help, and that of other churches, we were able to move from helping forty children at that time to over six hundred today.

Once Mark had clarity about the children and their needs, once he knew their names and the reasons the work was necessary, he gained the courage to undertake such a mission.

If we are to be courageous, we must get clear about what it is we are to do. Clarity raises the moral temperature in our lives that fuels courage. Clarity gives courage the power it needs to motivate us to act.

CLARITY GIVES COURAGE THE POWER IT NEEDS TO MOTIVATE US TO ACT.

CLEAR OUT IN NOWHERE

Jesus had clarity for himself. Luke tells us that Jesus was baptized in the Jordan River by John the Baptist, his cousin, and was then led by the Holy Spirit into the wilderness. I have been to the wilderness just beyond the Jordan River and I have a word to describe it: hot. Not just any hot. It can be energy-sucking, arid, searing hot. And I was there in November, when it was supposed to be mild. Even if Jesus went into the desert in the winter months when the heat was not an issue, there are some other words to describe it: desolate, wild, and forsaken. From the area north of where the Jordan River empties into the Dead Sea, if you look to the east, you can see caves in the hillsides. The rock desert before you is so barren that these caves, even from a distance, look like luxury condos. To step into this desert with the intention of seeking God for any period of time, much less forty days, took real nerve. We don't know how he survived there for more than a month. The Gospel writers offer us no insight into how Jesus found water, food, or firewood. We don't know if he had to deal with dangerous animals. All we know is that Jesus stayed in that area for forty days and nights. How he survived is not nearly as important as why he went in the first place. Jesus went there to gain final clarity about the mission of his life.

Jesus's wilderness experience is often associated with the word *temptation*. Whenever you seek clarity of purpose from God, the evil one will be happy to offer you alternatives. We know that Satan made some interesting offers to Jesus there.

"Turn this stone into bread. Let's see what you've got, kid!"

"Throw yourself off this high place; God has your back!"

"If you join my team today, I'll give you every kingdom you can see and a wonderful retirement package!"

Jesus quotes verse after verse of Scripture to reject the tempter's offers.

I have preached a lot of sermons on this passage. Like most, I talk about what Jesus teaches us when he rejects these offers of self-sufficiency, self-promotion, and self-aggrandizement. In these sermons, pastors often talk about how hard it would be to reject such opportunities. The thought is that it would be difficult for any of us; and Jesus, as one who was fully divine and fully human, would not have been exempt from the struggle. Anguished moments are imagined. Conflicted thoughts are perceived. The weariness and exhaustion produced by this desert experience could only enhance the desire to eat the bread, jump from the building, or become decadently rich and powerful.

But what if Jesus was actually just kind of bored? What if he answers these questions not with an anguished response of a man staring at the object of secret longings that he knows he has but should not seek, but rather, with a big, slow yawn? An immense drowsy mouth-stretch. What if his main response to the final enticement is one of those yawns that sucks flies off their flight paths, a yawn so lengthy that you have plenty of time to lift your hand to your gaping pie-hole because you are just so very b-o-r-e-d with what is being proposed to you? I suggest this because it is evident that Satan simply does not get Jesus. There is not a lot of back-and-forth in the text. Jesus swats these temptations away not with a lengthy debate based on a deep dive into Leviticus, but with a fast verse quotation of the sort you might hear in a third-grade Sunday school Bible recitation contest. Jesus has no angst. We do not hear him say, "I really want to have what you are offering here, but I know I shouldn't!" There is no back-and-forth, no anguished words or tormented mind. Sometimes Jesus doesn't even use a whole verse to say, "Thanks for coming out here and all, but I am just not even close to interested in what you are proposing."

Jesus is out in the wilderness to get clear and focused on what he will accomplish in the future. The great thing about knowing what you are about is that you also realize what you are not about. You understand what is attractive to you in life, but you also gain clarity about where the distractions are. You see with greater clarity which paths look inviting but are actually dead ends and the alluring spaces that seemed right but were actually tow-away zones. These temptations are nonstarters for Jesus. He knows his purpose and will not trade his birthright for a bowl of stew. Jesus says no to Satan because everything the evil one offers is so clearly outside the bounds of anything that interests him. That is how clarity leads to courageous decisions and the ability to do hard things. What many people think is difficult is, to the person with clarity, easy. Such a person is able to decline such moments not because what is offered lacks potential reward, but because making that choice is rendered nonsensical by the light of clarity.

THE POWER OF THE SPIRIT

Clarity not only initiates courage in the present, but it also helps sustain courage over the course of time. This is why Jesus took time to prayerfully give final consideration to the ministry he would undertake in the years that followed his time in the wilderness. Gaining clarity can feel like a wilderness experience when we are tired of thinking, worn out by options, and even spiritually dry. The arid nature of the wilderness, however, leaves one thinking about these essential things necessary not only for survival, but to begin to thrive in life. The longer we walk in a wilderness, the clearer the things we long for the most become. Jesus used this as a space to pray, be silent, and think. When we make time to be alone and think deeply and prayerfully, we create the opportunity for God to reboot our system. Few of us can get away alone anywhere for forty days. In your life, the quiet space to think may be a closed door with a sign that says, "Do not knock unless there is fire or blood." For some it is a long walk on a beach or the mountain vista after a long hike. Others take annual retreats for this purpose. It can be as simple as a couple of hours in a park, lying on the grass while you take in the sky and clouds. Wherever that place is that helps you go deep and prayerfully to consider the next step, the right move, the what-if, or to identify what simply must end, it is important to find it. When you take time to gain clarity about your purpose, you will be far more likely to exercise the courage necessary to do the things you dream of doing.

The more Jesus thinks and plans, the more excited he becomes and the more courage he gains. Think about the possible ending Luke could have recorded about Jesus's forty days in the wilderness. I would expect exhaustion, not excitement. We can imagine Luke writing, "Jesus returned from the wilderness on a stretcher carried by a few friends. He was dehydrated, famished, fatigued, and grateful to have survived the ordeal for forty days before he was found by the search party."

Now look at what the time in the wilderness actually did for Jesus. Luke records,

> Jesus, filled with the power of the Spirit, returned to Galilee, and a report about him spread through all the surrounding country. He began to teach in their synagogues and was praised by everyone.
>
> (Luke 4:14-15)

Luke wants us to understand that Jesus returned **with the power of the Spirit**. That is the source of his clarity. Jesus is fired up. He is on top of the world. He is kicking it. He is excited to share out what he has discerned when he went deep in. When you are absolutely certain that you know what you are about, the fifty miles you have to travel to get back to your hometown of Nazareth becomes an easy stride. This is the moment that he will begin the ministry we associate with his life and messiahship. He goes back to the synagogue in which he was raised, with the people who have known him since he was a child, to inaugurate his ministry. We can imagine that people smiled as he entered the synagogue. These are neighbors, friends, and members of his family. They gave him the task of reading the Scripture and maybe saying a few words. They have watched him grow up. They already know the authority in his voice when he reads Scripture and the gift he has at interpreting it.

Jesus read Isaiah 61:1-2:

> "The Spirit of the Lord is upon me,
>   because he has anointed me
>   to bring good news to the poor.
> He has sent me to proclaim release to the captives
>   and recovery of sight to the blind,

to let the oppressed go free,
to proclaim the year of the Lord's favor."
(Luke 4:18-19)

Then he said something no one expected, and no one seemed to like. When he sat down, he looked at them all and said, "Today this scripture has been fulfilled in your hearing" (Luke 4:21).

Think of how different the reading sounded in their ears after Jesus told them that the scripture was fulfilled in their hearing. I think when he added that declarative statement, they understood he was saying,

"The Spirit of the Lord is upon **ME**,
because he has anointed **ME**
to bring good news to the poor.
He has sent **ME** to proclaim release to the captives
and recovery of sight to the blind,
to let the oppressed go free,
to proclaim the year of the Lord's favor."
(Luke 4:18-19, emphasis added)

The impact was immediate. They begin a testy back-and-forth. Lacking the ability to politely send snarky text messages to one another, people began to mutter, *Who does he think he is?* Jesus basically replies, "I am less a carpenter like my dad, and more a prophet sent from God."

This is not what they were expecting. Like us, they probably hoped their town synagogue and its worship would be a shelter from everything that happened in the world. They wanted the synagogue to be a place where things calm down, not spin up. They didn't anticipate Jesus's next sentence about the prophecy being fulfilled today because rarely does anyone expect anything this overtly scriptural and declarative to happen in worship. Worship is often an event where we are willing to hear what has happened in the past, but not where we want someone to proclaim what is happening right here and right now. Most people think of worship more as spa time and less like a place to receive marching orders or an announcement that God is on the move, here and now before us. The congregation stirred that day precisely because Jesus was so clear that he necessitated a choice. It is almost like he is telling them that they can get in on the ground floor of the kingdom of God. They were the first to hear about it. Unfortunately, that also means that they could be the first to join him and help usher in the world he described.

The problem is that the type of transformation Isaiah described in that text is one that many admired but few hoped to undertake. It is much easier and safer to believe that Jesus's proclamation is false. This allows us to safely proceed with our unchanged, untransformed lives in a comfortably unbothered world. This basic desire to keep things in the same motionless state of unfulfilled biblical prophecy may be the reason that everyone was disturbed when Jesus said, "Today this scripture has been fulfilled in your hearing."

THE COURAGE OF CLARITY

Have you ever gotten the feeling that people who don't have faith in Jesus just don't have the risk threshold that allows them to believe in the world he describes or do what he says? Jesus turns your world upside down, and many would rather split hairs over theology or review the many mistakes and atrocities Jesus's followers have made over the centuries rather than even consider what Jesus himself calls us to do and be. How might we share our faith differently if we thought that the biggest obstacle to Christian belief was fear rather than doubt?

I wonder if the hometown crowd felt fear when Jesus said he was a prophet on the order of Elijah. The audacity of this comparison and the clear vision Jesus had to bless the poor and oppressed disrupted those who heard it. Resistance should be expected when we share a clear understanding of important work that must be done. They transitioned from hometown crowd to angry mob very quickly. The animosity in the synagogue spread fast in both speed and intensity. They made a decision. They decided to throw Jesus off a cliff.

You will need courage when you become clear about how you see the world. Often people will not like it. They are more likely to want to kill your dream than kill you. This will be done by telling you that it is wrong, impossible, a bad idea, harmful to the organization, and a ridiculous notion. Fear motivates people to tear down rather than build up. Your clarity will be seen by some as troublemaking. As you describe a needed change in the life of an individual or community that you plan to pursue, others will understand that it may require them to sacrifice something they deem important or embrace a difficult task themselves. Even if a person or organization desperately needs to change to avoid failure, divorce, or bankruptcy, or to seize new opportunities, people tend to do whatever it takes to hold fast to the current state of play. Failure is not pleasant, but it may be so pleasantly familiar that people will readily choose it over all the good you describe in your calling.

FEAR MOTIVATES PEOPLE TO TEAR DOWN RATHER THAN BUILD UP. YOUR CLARITY WILL BE SEEN BY SOME AS TROUBLEMAKING.

The easiest way to silence a person who has achieved clarity about what he or she must do is to show the person the many reasons the thing cannot be done. It is necessary to describe the obstacles as they really are, but also to make each one into a ten-foot giant that stands like Goliath before the army of Israel. The more the giant taunts, the more the courage of the personnel in the army melts away. Soon there is no able-bodied person willing to face the Goliath. When the clarity of purpose is offered, reason after reason is given for why everything described is simply impossible. The fearful will soon begin to say, "You don't have that ability. You've never been that smart. People will never support it. The budget could never be reallocated. People don't want this change. Some people simply cannot change. That is against our policy handbook. You are unrealistic. You are uninformed. You have lost your mind."

One by one the fear giants are released until you are tempted to lose your courage, your clarity, and your calling.

OUSADO MEANS DARING

Fear giants can overtake us because we carry a framework of fear about many things in life. The button on my desk is one that I was given at an international assembly of nearly one thousand delegates of my denomination. The button was at my seat when I arrived before a week of meetings that I knew would be contentious. I noticed that there were a variety of words on the buttons at the seats of other delegates. Mine read *Ousado*. A quick search on my phone told me that *Ousado* is Portuguese for "Daring." I thought, "This is a message from God. Be daring!"

I found this harder than it sounded. It would be great if wearing a pin made you daring and courageous. Often I do not feel daring. Some days I feel like someone attached another pin to my back that reads:

Temeroso." That is the Portuguese word for "afraid" or "fearful." These words are important in any language because they denote a default setting of caution that we often carry. This is the reason that, when someone gets really clear about her or his calling to change something in that person's life or in the world, resistance will emerge.

That is what happens in the synagogue in Nazareth in Luke 4:28-29. Jesus declares his intention to change how the world worked. He redefines what is important in life as he talks about the good news he plans to bring. His words must have sounded revolutionary to those who heard them. Jesus was saying that the old order of things, a world that was full of the assumption of dislike and distrust between people based on their race, ability, and economic or social class would now be perpetually challenged. Jesus was bringing the world a hunger for justice in our relationships with each other and in society at large. He was including those who had been rejected. He was exalting those who had been held down.

In a normal worship service, Jesus announced that the reign of God was about to end the reign of everything and everybody else. Naturally they wanted to throw him off a cliff. It was a lot to take in. It was disruptive.

They march him up the hill, but Jesus is not buying into fear. He is not caught up in their anxiety. Jesus does not fight against them, apologize, or pander to the crowd. He does not need their support or approval. He is free in the best sense of the word. Luke tells us that "he passed through the midst of them and went on his way" (Luke 4:30).

This courage will be a necessary trait of Jesus's character and life because what he describes will require tremendous sacrifice to accomplish. Make no mistake, there is a direct line between Jesus's statement in his home synagogue where he states that he will fulfill

Isaiah's prophecy, his teaching about the kingdom of God being an experience where the hungry are filled with good things while the rich are sent away empty, and his death on a cross. Jesus knows what his life and ministry are about. He states things plainly. He is consistent in his message.

As the crowds were drawn to the clarity of his preaching, he created a greater threat to those who were in power. Jesus died for many reasons, most notably to reconcile humanity to God; but the context of that death is one of conflict with religious and political powers who believed that the message he proclaimed was dangerous to the positions and security that they held.

FIND YOUR MAGNIFICENCE

Have you thought about what your life is about lately? You may be a person in a unique season of life. You need to finish your education. You have a child to raise. You are considering what to do in retirement. You have a demanding job. You grieve the loss of a loved one. You celebrate the arrival of a newborn. Each person is different, in diverse seasons of life with vastly different circumstances. Everyone is also the same. If you spend a little time in the wilderness and figure out what the next three months or the next three years is about, you will be able to take hold of the opportunities present in this moment with courage. When either your inner voice or other people try to discourage you with fear or point out all the reasons that you cannot do what is before you, clarity of purpose will call out the courage that will enable you to pass through the midst of them and go on your way.

Thomas Aquinas, a theologian in the thirteenth century, had a word for the clarity a person could have about the good she or he was called to do in life. He called it your *magnificence*. He believed that such clarity was essential to courage because it would make the personal risk and sacrifice that a calling requires worth enduring if the outcome could be achieved. When the calling a person identifies is something the Holy Spirit prompted them to hear, it becomes even more likely that they will demonstrate courage. Courage is easier to exhibit when we know we are in communion with God and the company of others. When a person is clear that she or he serves the larger purposes of God in the world, that person also gains the trust that she or he is empowered by the Holy Spirit to do so. This is why time spent in spiritual disciplines like prayer, study of the Scripture, worship, or silence is essential to this task. We are far more likely to undertake necessary courageous actions when we return in the power of the Holy Spirit to do what the Holy Spirit has directed in our lives. Such work is your *magnificence*. You are magnifying the presence of God through the efforts of your life the calling directs.

Use this word in a sentence. Consider the main thing that you believe your life to be about for the coming year. Write that down. Then add, *will be my magnificence*. Here are some examples:

- *Caring for my parents will be my magnificence.*
- *Building a business that serves the community and our employees will be my magnificence.*
- *Helping our town expand affordable housing will be my magnificence.*
- *Learning how to raise our children well will be my magnificence.*
- *Refurbishing the park for kids in our neighborhood will be my magnificence.*

- *Being a better friend will be my magnificence.*
- *Finding a new job where I can best use my training will be my magnificence.*
- *Helping my students read at grade level will be my magnificence.*
- *Joining others to renew our church is my magnificence.*

I wonder if Jesus gained some of the clarity about his life from his mother, Mary. When Mary learned she was to be the mother of the Messiah, she offered the Magnificat. Portions of Mary's song clearly foreshadow Jesus's ministry and message.

> "His mercy is for those who fear him
>   from generation to generation.
> He has shown strength with his arm;
>   he has scattered the proud in the thoughts of
>   their hearts.
> He has brought down the powerful from their
> thrones,
>   and lifted up the lowly;
> he has filled the hungry with good things,
>   and sent the rich away empty."
>
> (Luke 1:50-53)

Mary speaks of the mercy of God who scatters the proud and pulls the powerful from their thrones while the lowly are lifted up. The rich are sent away empty while the hungry are filled with good things. The reversal that happens when the kingdom of God enters the world casts aside the old order of things and makes all things new. Mary had her own magnificence. It was the vision she gained when the angel asked if she would bear the Christ Child and be his mother. Imagine how being raised by a mother with such clarity about the way God would have the world work impacted the life of Jesus. He heard her speak of this when he was a child. It was the basis of formative conversation when he was an adolescent. Mary fed the flame of righteousness until it burned bright and hot.

Make no mistake, your magnificence inspires courage not only in your life, but in the lives of those around you. Your clarity becomes their clarity. It is a gift to your children. It is the beauty your friends see in your life and that blesses their own. Likewise, when you lack this sense of clarity of calling in life, you are uniquely unable to influence others to see the world as God describes it in Holy Scripture.

MAKE NO MISTAKE, YOUR MAGNIFICENCE INSPIRES COURAGE NOT ONLY IN YOUR LIFE, BUT IN THE LIVES OF THOSE AROUND YOU.

THE BELOVED COMMUNITY

From time to time there arises a person whose clarity about his or her purpose enables us to see that the word *magnificence* is not overstated. Representative John Lewis lived such a life, working to create what he and others in the Civil Rights Movement called "The Beloved Community" in the United States. He was born the son of sharecroppers on February 21, 1940, near Troy, Alabama, during the height of Jim Crow segregation in the United States.[1] He attended the segregated schools in Pike County, Alabama, which received meager funding and resources compared to schools for white children. He first heard the principles of The Beloved Community while listening to the Reverend Martin Luther King, Jr. on the radio. When he heard King speak, Lewis knew that he wanted to join a movement that wanted to *"confront the erroneous belief that some of us are more valuable or important than others, and demonstrate the truth of human equality."* [2]

Lewis said, *"When I heard King it was as though a light turned on in my heart. When I heard his voice I felt he was talking directly to me."* [3] Lewis did not catch someone else's dream. He saw the magnificence of the Civil Rights Movement as a whole, including nonviolent protest, agitation, deep learning about the history of race, and the call to see the promised kingdom of God present on the earth in a society that was based on equity and justice for all. Lewis went to Nashville to attend college. Soon he was organizing sit-in demonstrations. Pictures show him being carried to a police wagon by two police officers after he failed to obey orders to leave a whites-only segregated restaurant. He led the Freedom Riders, who challenged segregated transportation across the South, sitting in seats that were reserved for white passengers. Everywhere John Lewis went, his clear understanding of how the world should be gave him the courage to face hardships at every turn. He was beaten, arrested, chased by angry mobs, and a victim of police brutality who refused to give up until Jim Crow segregation was a thing of the past. Lewis was only twenty-three years old when he stood at the Lincoln Memorial and was a keynote speaker during the March on Washington in the summer of 1963. [4]

Many would say that John Lewis had a surplus of courage, which enabled him to endure the hardships that came with his work. This would miss the more important movement in his life. Before he had courage, he had clarity about how the world should be and what he would have to do to gain such a world for himself or bring it to others. This clarity came from a deep and abiding faith in Christ and a knowledge of God's love for all people that he could read clearly in the

Bible. Lewis's faith in Christ enabled him to be prompted and led by the Holy Spirit to speak and act courageously. He knew that the vision he served was greater than one he could produce on his own. His was a biblical vision of the world, where all God's children were treated with equity and justice, and he walked with the Holy Spirit as he became one of the Big Six leaders of the Civil Rights Movement.

John Lewis died on July 17, 2020. On the day of his funeral, newspapers around the United States released an essay he wrote shortly before his death, to be published on the day of his funeral. In this essay, Lewis reminded readers that his clarity came when he heard the voice of Dr. Martin Luther King, Jr. on an old radio. Lewis wrote,

> Ordinary people with extraordinary vision can redeem the soul of America by getting in what I call good trouble, necessary trouble....Though I may not be here with you, I urge you to answer the highest calling of your heart and stand up for what you truly believe. In my life I have done all I can to demonstrate that the way of peace, the way of love and nonviolence is the more excellent way. Now it is your turn to let freedom ring.[5]

Courage is not the rare attribute of a small set of great men and women who are more daring or braver than the rest of us. It is the gift God gives ordinary people when we seek a clear vision of what God would have us do throughout our lives, or at this moment and time in our lives. If you want to be courageous, take time to find clarity of purpose, or clarity about what is really going on in your life, society, and the world. Seek the will of the Holy Spirit and then begin to act. You may be surprised at how an ordinary person like you can find what Lewis called "good trouble, necessary trouble" or how you can offer peace and healing to the lives of many.

Chapter 2

THE CONVICTION
OF COURAGE

[Jesus] was teaching in one of the synagogues
on the sabbath. And just then there appeared
a woman with a spirit that had crippled her for
eighteen years. She was bent over and was quite
unable to stand up straight. When Jesus saw her,
he called her over and said, "Woman, you are set
free from your ailment." When he laid his hands on
her, immediately she stood up straight and began
praising God. But the leader of the synagogue,
indignant because Jesus had cured on the sabbath,
kept saying to the crowd, "There are six days on
which work ought to be done; come on those days
and be cured, and not on the sabbath day." But the

Lord answered him and said, "You hypocrites! Does not each of you on the sabbath untie his ox or his donkey from the manger, and lead it away to give it water? And ought not this woman, a daughter of Abraham whom Satan bound for eighteen long years, be set free from this bondage on the sabbath day?" When he said this, all his opponents were put to shame; and the entire crowd was rejoicing at all the wonderful things that he was doing.

(Luke 13:10-17)

Jesus entered a synagogue on the sabbath. When most of us enter a place of worship as a visitor, we make our way through the regular attendees and try to find a seat. This is typically done in a cautious manner. We don't want to take the seat of one of the regulars. We all know that when you gather at a place of worship, everyone is supposed to be friendly and welcoming. We also know that people have their seats and you don't want to be the person who takes anyone's seat. We see people in the light of our desire to not offend. We want to make sure someone will not feel the need to come stake her or his claim. While I don't think Jesus had those concerns, this was the scene. In the midst of this, Jesus saw the woman bent over from eighteen years of infirmity.

When Jesus sees this, he makes a decision. I think he knows that this decision will come with a price. In this case, Jesus knew that his action might lead to a reaction in the synagogue. Technically, healing a person—or doing any work—on the sabbath was out of bounds. I imagine him taking that deep breath that you take right before you do something that you are fully aware other people may not like, but you are committed to do anyway. This is how courage works. Courage causes us to take the initiative. Courage is necessary to overcome fear. Often we do not act because we fear how others will perceive us, whether we will upset someone or be judged. When Jesus sees the woman whose spine is so bent that she is stooped over as she walks, he knows it is worth the risk. Jesus calls the woman over and, right there in front of God and everybody, declares her free of her disorder. This was an act of healing that was fully consistent with the vow he made in his home synagogue in Nazareth to set the oppressed free. The woman, able to stand straight for the first time in eighteen years, began to praise God.

That is when the trouble began. We all like the stories of courage where the hero saves the day. We tend not to think about the price the hero pays. When you do something courageous, there may be a price. In this moment, it is a leader of the synagogue, frustrated that Jesus may have violated the law by doing a miracle on the sabbath. It is important to note that courage is disruptive in any circumstance. It will be disruptive to your life and disruptive to people around you. Rather than honor this synagogue leader's indignation with an apology or walk back a miracle by asking if it would be all right if he straightened her up just a degree or two until the sun went down on the sabbath, Jesus speaks out on her behalf.

We know how hard it is to disagree with the majority, especially when someone says something strongly. It is easier to examine the buckle on your sandal and hope it will all settle down. It is likely that Jesus is experiencing some cognitive dissonance. This lovely woman is standing upright for the first time and no one joins her celebration. They are in the synagogue, and no one offers a prayer of thanksgiving. This may be why, when Jesus calls them hypocrites, he uses an exclamation point. Hypocrites! Think about it, how often do people ever use an exclamation point in a house of worship? Many churches got rid of their exclamation points years ago. Exclamation points take courage because they disrupt the polite calm as they note something important. They enable us to hear and see conviction.

In this moment of conflict, Jesus teaches us something about courage. Courage arises from the God-inspired convictions we hold about how the world should work and what we should do to care for and support others. Jesus teaches us that it is important, even necessary, to hold conviction that is rooted in God's love and mercy. Jesus shows us that we must not defer from action for fear of conflict. When God calls, it is no time to avert your eyes or hope it was intended for someone else.

> **COURAGE ARISES FROM THE GOD-INSPIRED CONVICTIONS WE HOLD ABOUT HOW THE WORLD SHOULD WORK AND WHAT WE SHOULD DO TO CARE FOR AND SUPPORT OTHERS.**

FAITH AND CONVICTION

As we see in this Scripture passage, courage overcomes doubt and fear. It enables us to maintain our faith in the ultimate expression of God's presence, which is love, and initiate action.

Much of courage lies in the willingness to act, especially when we know that our actions may be criticized by others and may not immediately lead to the outcome that we desire. Courageous people maintain an abiding conviction that the calling of Christ's love they pursue and the actions they undertake are meaningful and worthwhile in the eyes of God. They have faith that what they are doing is worth the criticism endured and the sacrifice required. They also understand that just because they act with courage does not mean that everything will work out fine. Faith is therefore necessary to their effort. They hold faith not in their own capacity or skill, or even in the personal effort courage evokes from them. They hold faith in the way God has created the world and the desire to serve a higher purpose. When Jesus healed the woman in the synagogue, he was performing an act of kindness that fulfilled the calling shared by the prophet Micah,

> "He has told you, O mortal, what is good;
> and what does the LORD require of you
> but to do justice, and to love kindness,
> and to walk humbly with your God?"
> (Micah 6:8)

Micah describes not what he hopes we will do. He does not offer his best advice on how we should act. Here Micah describes how the world works. Micah observes three foundational pillars that God has laid under all human relationships. When we act in justice, kindness, and humility toward God and others, we find a good life. When we do not, we find frustration, resentment, and indignation. Micah is not telling us that we need to create justice, kindness, and humility. God has already done so. Micah simply describes the life of a person who is right with God. Such a person will have faith in the goodness of God described here. She or he will also have the conviction to live life in a way that express justice, kindness, and humility. The faith such a person holds leads to the conviction that he or she not only believes but enacts. In this way, such a person will conform his or her life to the aspects of God's goodness that the person sees and admires.

A person's faith is an assent to the principles of God's righteousness found in Scripture. The ability to not only see God's ways and desire them, but actually hunger and thirst for righteousness, is the beginning of faith that leads to courage. Jesus obviously wanted to move his followers from faith as a general agreement or ascent to truth, to an experience akin to hunger and thirst. This type of faith and conviction is a sustained longing that drives decisions and actions. Just as a thirsty person is consumed with a search for water, so one who thirsts for God's righteousness will work until she or he finds some form of resolution in keeping with the calling God has placed on that person's heart. This conviction of the worthiness of God's ways is faith. Conviction about God's righteousness allows persons to conform their life to this reality. When we are convicted to be in concert with the ways of God, courage will be evoked in our lives. Bland agreement with Scripture that is void of sufficient conviction to act is a form of cowardice at best and disobedience at worst.

Courage in a faith-centered life is not a linear movement from faith to conviction to action. It is cyclical. Faith leads to conviction that leads to action that leads to faith again. With sustained courage, this pattern repeats itself, allowing us to move from being a part of courageous actions to being in the flow of courageous movements over time. Some think that faith is a speculative bet on something we hope will come true. That is not true. Faith is the assurance we carry about what God has already done and is now doing in the pattern that begins to form our life in Christ. Faith is what we know we will see and experience not because of our efforts, but because of the assurance we have of who God is, as one whose ways are trustworthy, right, and true. This is another form of conviction that propels us down the often uncertain and risky path on which courage leads us. Sometimes it seems we will never reach the end as we walk through trees, shrubs, and topography that currently limit our view. If we continue to take faithful, courageous steps, the journey leads us to vistas where we see more clearly a panoramic view of the nature of God, in all of its beauty.

Such a journey is impossible when courage is absent. The terrain is too difficult. The hills are too high and the air too hot and humid. The journey is simply not worth the effort to many people. The virtue of courage never demonstrates itself in the tepid belief systems of Christians who intellectually agree with Scripture and the doctrine of the church, but who do not hunger and thirst to see the kingdom of God actually manifest itself in the lives of people in their family, community, and nation.

HOW CONVICTION LEADS TO COURAGE

There are many ways to develop and discover a Christ-centered conviction. Start by paying attention to the moment that God gets your attention through anger, longing, or urgency. When you find yourself in the heart of these emotions, stop and listen.

Embrace Your Anger

It is hard to think that anger could be a good thing. Many feel battered by the anger they experience in so many places, from the words of national leaders to the social media expressions of their friends. Anger is all the rage these days, and it has torn the fabric of our relationships and encouraged us to be our lesser selves, people who are mean, rude, or seek personal gain as they make a scene and insist on their own way. YouTube videos of people saying and doing outrageous things to get what they want are commonplace.

That is not the anger I am talking about.

Pay attention to righteous anger. Prophets, leaders, and common people who did courageous things in the Bible are those who could differentiate righteous anger motivated by God and harmful anger motivated by ego and self-focus. Righteous anger is rarely evoked by something that happens to you. It is often experienced when you see people doing something out of order with the will of God. It has an element of deep compassion for the negative impact the unfairness and injustice has on vulnerable people. It seeks to repair damage done when some are acting outside the boundaries of God's goodness. Jesus exhibited righteous anger when he saw the Temple in Jerusalem treated as a marketplace. Jesus does not personally benefit from what he is doing. He acts out of a sense of frustration that the primary place of worship of God is being violated for the monetary gain of a group of vendors (Luke 19:45-46).

When you see some form of injustice, and it gives you an unmistakable sense that it is just not right and something needs to be done, God is trying to evoke courage in you. Conviction feels much like anger. Blood pressure is raised. Adrenaline is released. Muscles tense. Focus narrows. While it is important to recognize that a good bit of prayer and a couple of sanity checks from wise friends are always in order before one takes action, the experience of righteous anger is often a sign that God is tapping you on the shoulder and wants you to act.

On a mission trip to Sierra Leone, Africa, days after the peace treaty between the government and rebel forces who had committed numerous war crimes and atrocities, our team was in a camp full of refugees who had to flee their villages and homes. These people had used mud to make brick dwellings that were being protected from the severe downpours of the rainy season by worn United Nations relief tarps. People were friendly and grateful to see us when they learned we offered medical care. Our small team included two doctors and a nurse who offered vaccinations and medical care. Despite a good deal of planning, we realized that our supplies were very limited and the line of those seeking aid was very long.

Most of the people who came suffered with ailments that were easy to diagnose and care for with medicine that we had gathered and brought with us. By the end of the day, all the medicine had been handed out and the sun was going down over the small, unlit building we were using. Our host quietly asked us to climb through the window and discreetly get in the waiting van he had pulled up to the side of the building. He wanted us to leave in a way that would keep people still standing in line from hurting one another in an attempt to be seen. He knew, and they knew, that no other medical clinic would be offered in the foreseeable future.

As we drove away, the crowd began to yell for us. Some people ran after our van. I felt many emotions. Among them was anger that so many people would have such deep needs and lack any access to simple medicine widely available in so many other places in the world. Another was compassion for the needs people carried daily in that place. There was no van coming to whisk them away to a better life. That sense of righteous anger and God-inspired compassion was shared by one of the doctors on that trip. That week our group continually returned to talk about that experience. We asked what we were to do in light of Christ's clear teaching about caring for the sick and those in need. For the next several years it drove our conversation and work with many others. After years of work, Mercy Hospital, a medical facility in Bo, Sierra Leone, opened. Mercy's mission has a focus on maternal and child health and serves people, even when they cannot afford to pay the standard fees. There is a direct line from that moment of compassion and anger over the realization of the inadequacy of a one-day clinic and the creation of a hospital run by professionals in Sierra Leone that is open all year long. The entire journey has been an experience of courage as we have been repeatedly convicted to take risks, find new ways to work with our partners in Sierra Leone, and find innovative ways to serve vulnerable people in ways pleasing to Christ.

Many things in this world evoke righteous anger in the lives of people who hunger and thirst for righteousness. It is remarkable that we are often so fearful of conflict or discomfort that we choose to look away rather than feel distressed over what is before our eyes. A hungry child should elicit compassion, but she or he should also inspire some modicum of anger. Boys, girls, and adolescents sold into sex trafficking to bring profit should make our anger spill over into action. When you become outraged as you watch a video of a police officer in Minnesota kneel on the neck of George Floyd, a handcuffed African American man, until he dies of asphyxiation, it is a sign that God is doing something in your heart. When we experience righteous anger, it is often this type of cry against injustice. If you are uncomfortable with such heightened emotions, do not be concerned. The feeling of outrage the video evokes is a sign that something is right with you. It is a visceral form of Jesus's call to hunger and thirst for righteousness.

Let Longing Lead You

There is a woman in the Bible who probably longed for a different life. Her name was Mary. We often call her Mary Magdalene. Magdala was the name of her town, a prosperous community on the north end of the Sea of Galilee. Mary had a very hard life. When Luke introduces Mary Magdalene in his Gospel, he offers some rather remarkable information about her life: "Jesus went on through cities and villages, proclaiming and bringing the good news of the kingdom of God. The twelve were with him, as well as some women who had been cured of evil spirits and infirmities: Mary, called Magdalene, from whom seven demons had gone out..." (Luke 8:1-2).

Seven demon sounds like a lot to me. Actually, when you deal with demons, any number over zero sounds like a lot. We don't know exactly how those demons manifested themselves. We don't know if Mary suffered seven different physical ailments, or seven different forms of mental illness, or if they produced different types of dysfunctional behavior in her life. All we know for sure is that clearly, seven demons is not a good thing.

Mary probably had to deal with what people in her community said about her as she dealt with her demons. Some people love to talk about the problems of others and offer simple solutions that will clean everything up in a jiffy. They then offer judgment about what the person is not doing, and so easily could do, that leads to their continued decline. People, and by this, I mean church people, have speculated and promulgated a good bit of slander about Mary Magdalene, conflating her with other women in the Bible and suggesting, with no evidence in the text, that she was a prostitute. But here we are dealing with the Mary Magdalene who is actually presented in the Bible. There is very little we know about her other than her seven demons and her healing by Jesus.

Mary probably felt captive to her condition for many years. I would guess that she longed for more in life. I wonder if she had that voice in her head that told her that she could not overcome these problems or have a normal life. Many people have an inner voice that tries to convince them not to reach out to others, not to be a burden, and to get their act together. This voice tells you that the good you long for is not possible, that while God made everything and called it good, you are the exception. It is the voice that tells you that God does not watch you, care for you, or has lost interest in the messy parts of your life. It takes courage to quiet that voice.

At some point Mary gained enough faith in Jesus to elicit the courage to seek help from him. We know that she turned to Jesus and was healed by him, because Luke talks about the demons in the past tense. Her longing to be whole and well creates the conviction that enables her to either ask Jesus for help or just say "yes" when he offers it. I picture that scene. She is in distress. She is ready for another disappointment. She must have been tired of dealing with the problems and the gossip it created. While she is burdened, Jesus is excited. He can see her worth in ways she cannot imagine. Jesus knows that her demons are no match for him. Jesus is clear about his mission. He is here to bring liberty to the oppressed. People who were castoffs, people that others said were beyond hope because they were possessed by demons, people who thought their history would determine their future, were all people that Jesus uniquely cared about, healed, and set free.

That is good news for anyone who wants to find courage in his or her life. The truth is that we are a lot like Mary. I bet you have what may feel like a demon or two in your own life that you want to see tossed out. You may have wrestled with something that came out of nowhere and felt larger than your capacity to manage. Further, I bet someone, or a group of someones, has said things about you that were as hurtful as they were untrue. Like Mary, you may have a longing to become more than you are right now. It is similar to the anger you may feel when you see the world as it is and long for it to be more. The unfairness of your circumstances may even anger you. That longing is the key to the conviction that unlocks courage in a person's life. You are far more likely to do the courageous things that lead to transformation when you actively long for the state of being the change would bring.

Mary found this transformation and became one of Jesus's followers. She was able to hear Jesus teach about life in the kingdom of God. She saw him do other miracles. Luke tells us that she and the other women had the ability to support Jesus and the disciples out of their own means. In the first century, this fact alone speaks of a remarkable group of women. Not only do they have the means to provide support, but they are also committed to this worthy pursuit. They use their resources to advance the ministry of Christ, so that others will experience the healing and transformation they have undergone. Mary was present when Jesus taught the crowds and healed the sick. Undoubtedly, she shared her testimony of healing with others. Why is it that Mary overcame seven demons when we often struggle to control one bad habit? The answer is probably found in the question of how much we long for real change. That longing creates conviction. And conviction is necessary to elicit the courage that makes action possible.

CONVICTION IS NECESSARY TO ELICIT THE COURAGE THAT MAKES ACTION POSSIBLE.

Know What Is Truly Urgent

Sometimes when we say *urgent*, we mean something that might actually be inconsequential—an urgent email, an urgent conversation, or an urgent need to clean your computer keyboard when you are supposed to be typing a report. The kind of urgency I'm talking about here, though, is the important kind. A visit to the emergency room is truly urgent. The rescue of someone dangling from a cliff, or weeping in suicidal peril, or dying of hunger in a far-off place—these represent the kind of urgency that simply cannot wait.

Often a moment of conviction arises because the need is obvious, what is at stake is essential, and the time to act is immediate. That was the situation of a Roman centurion. A powerful man, he had no way to help a servant so sick that he might die. The centurion heard about Jesus's ability and had faith he could heal this servant. He sought the help of the local Jewish elders of his community. Perhaps he feared that Jesus would not help a member of the army that currently occupied his country. He was not sure about Jesus, but he was sure that he was desperate and apparently convicted that Jesus was his only hope. The elders agreed to approach Jesus. They described the centurion as someone who was a part of their community and who had built the local synagogue. Jesus agreed to come and began the journey to his home. The centurion believed he was unworthy to be in the presence of such a great rabbi and healer. Further, his conviction about Jesus's power led him to believe that Jesus didn't need to make the journey to his house anyway. When he heard Jesus was on his way, he sent friends with a message: "Lord, don't be bothered. I don't deserve to have you come under my roof. In fact, I didn't even consider myself worthy to come to you. Just say the word and my servant will be healed" (Luke 7:6b-7 CEB).

Jesus was impressed. He turned to the people following him and said, "I tell you, even in Israel I haven't found faith like this" (Luke 7:9b CEB).

Desperation is motivational. The more conviction the centurion held about Jesus's capacity and his servant's need, the more courage grew, and the more willing he was to enlist his friends to help him make a bold request of Jesus. It saved the servant's life.

The centurion found himself in a situation that was truly urgent. He had to do what he could in a very short time, and out of this urgency was born the courage and conviction for him to do whatever he had to do to help his servant.

HOW COURAGE WILL FIND YOU

As we experience anger, longing, or urgency, we find that, in many ways, courage has found us more than we find courage. God has used these experiences to gain our attention so that we can work in concert with the will of the Holy Spirit. God is already at work in the world. We are not the point of origin for any good act. We join the Holy Spirit in the work that God is working to advance and accomplish. We have to find ways to move from conviction prompted by God to actions we undertake that we uniquely can do. The Holy Spirit knows us and wants to use our unique talents, training, strengths, and gifts. Conviction is calling them out in a moment so that we will act with courage. As we sustain such courage over time, we see the fruit that the seeds of conviction produce.

Get Serious

Christ-centered conviction by itself is of little use unless it is secured to self-discipline and a willingness to work. Most people have heard what sounds like conviction in the words a person who is impassioned about politics, social issues, ideology, or the fact that their neighbor does not take their trash can off the sidewalk in a timely manner as every decent human being in the world knows you should.

A fervent view should not be confused with the virtue of courage. Courage is uniquely displayed in the lives of serious people who do serious work on important matters. It is courageous to be the first person in your family to enter training in a trade that will provide a stable income or enroll in college to prepare for your career. To do so means that you have to get your act together. You have to study for the classes, do well on the tests, build your résumé, and demonstrate that you are ready to invest in yourself.

Several years ago, my nephew was choosing a college major. He was considering a career in law enforcement or national security. The church I serve has many people who work in a variety of governmental agencies related to such a career path. I set up a series of interviews with people in these fields so he could ask them questions. At the end of each conversation, they each separately reviewed things he would need to do to be a viable candidate. They told him to earn good grades, demonstrate leadership skills in sports or clubs. Each list varied a bit, but the last statement was the same. "Let me tell you what not to do. Do not get arrested on drug charges. If you do, you are out." After this happened the fifth time, my nephew turned to me and said, "Uncle Tom, did you put these people up to this?!"

I did not script any of those conversations. Instead, each person told my nephew that anyone who had a conviction to serve in their field had to get serious. When you are serious about the work, there are things you do, and there are things you do not do.

There is no habit that you cannot overcome, no situation that God cannot change, and no end to the potential of what you can accomplish when you get clear and convicted about what God has put before you. A cursory reading of Scripture will identify, however, that it has never been easy for people like Joseph, Moses, Deborah, David, Esther,

Jeremiah, Naomi, Paul, Stephen, Lydia, Timothy, or anyone else to do what God was asking them to do. You have to make plans, gather resources, find allies and friends, and work long and hard if you want to serve God in ways small or large that are significant.

It does not matter if you are raising a child or serving as principal of a school, whether you are the custodian in charge of sterilizing the operating room or the surgeon who will perform the surgery, all the work is important, and it belongs to those who get serious about getting the work done. It takes courage to show up day after day, overcome the obstacles, and after accomplishing one's goal, set new ones. Those who sustain their drive and passion over time understand that while courage sometimes only has to fill an adrenaline-filled moment, it is more likely to present itself in the sustained commitment of those who find a way to stand firm and continue a task when they are most tempted to walk away.

> **IT TAKES COURAGE TO SHOW UP DAY AFTER DAY, OVERCOME THE OBSTACLES, AND AFTER ACCOMPLISHING ONE'S GOAL, SET NEW ONES.**

Get Out of the Way

If you hunger and thirst for righteousness, it is important to go to the well that has living water rather than hope that your one-liter water bottle will be sufficient.

I have a sign some church members gave me, a sign that reads *Love Never Fails*. The words are found in 1 Corinthians 13:8, from the well-known chapter on love by the apostle Paul. Prophecies will cease, says Paul, tongues will be stilled, knowledge will pass away. Love never fails.

It is remarkable what three words convey. That sign was a reminder of another foundational pillar God has put in place. It speaks to the power of love God put in motion as a force that influences the events of humanity over time. If the arc of history bends toward justice, love is the force that is pushing on it to do so.

Months after I put this sign in its prominent space, another sign appeared. Other friends returned from a trip to Germany. They brought me a metal sign that read *Berlin*. I had been to Berlin myself and enjoyed the capital city a great deal. The people were friendly. The architecture was interesting. It exuded a complex and sometimes dark history that evoked a great deal of meaningful thought and conversation. Most of all, it was also a great place to take pictures of myself. When your name is Berlin and you happen to be in Berlin, you are, well, everywhere. I took my picture under every Berlin sign I could find. I set a personal record for selfies. I may have set a German record for selfies. I drove people around me crazy when I would stop again and say, "Wow, I really don't want to miss this opportunity to take my picture with this sign. Tom Berlin, here in Berlin, Germany, with this sign that reads 'Berlin.' Does it get better than this?"

They were pretty sure that it did, in fact, get better than this.

As you can imagine, when my friends gave me the sign from Berlin for a Berlin that read *Berlin*, I wanted to place it somewhere prominent, so that they would know of my appreciation. I quickly positioned it in front of the wood block that read *Love Never Fails*. I meant to move it to another location, but after they left, it remained there. I kept it there for months. I wonder now if there was something else going on other than convenience of sign placement. While *Love Never Fails* inspired me, it also caused me to question its truth. Love does sometimes fail. Marriages fail. Friendships fail. Peace treaties fail. There are many examples in world news and personal lives where love is not the victor. The longer that sign sat on that shelf, the longer my list of love fails inevitably grew. I wonder if that was why I grew comfortable seeing *Berlin* obstruct *Love Never Fails*.

Do you ever get in your own way?

What I describe here is not a crisis of faith, but a period of sloth in conviction about the ways of God. I was losing a degree of faith in the clarity of Paul's words. I held God responsible for the failure of the love of people. My disappointment was visible in the placement of those two signs. There will be times when love fails among people. But the love of God does not, will not, and cannot ultimately fail. One day I felt prompted to flip those two signs. I moved the *Berlin* out of the way and let *Love Never Fails* speak again. That was restorative. Since *Love Never Fails* retook the marquee position, it has served as a daily reminder that I need. I take courage and strength from that truth.

Have you ever noticed that when we get out of the way of our faith and conviction about God's ways, courage rises? Courage is a consistent virtue in our lives when we don't depend on our own capacity but instead on the truths that flow from our faith in God. Convicted of God's ability, we are able to love, forgive, attempt reconciliation, resist sin, stand up to injustice, care about the poor, be compassionate and kind.

Scale Up Courage

Years ago, my father was talking to an orthopedic physician about some difficulty he was having with his hand. During the appointment, he also identified a bump on his hand and asked if it was a problem. The doctor examined it and said that he had something similar on his own hand. He then shared that he had done some research about this particular type of bump and said, "that bump indicates that you are genetically connected to the Vikings." My dad called each of his sons soon after he left the doctor's office. "You will never believe what I learned. We are Vikings!"

I told him that, while I would like to learn more about the veracity of the science, this diagnosis did explain why I sometimes had the urge to pillage small towns when I drive down the interstate. The next time we were all together, our extended family decided to celebrate our newfound heritage by holding a Viking dinner. Everyone from the oldest great-grandparent to the youngest great-grandchild was admitted to the dinner table only when they wore garb that included a horned Viking hat, fake beard, vest, and a fierce look. My father presented each of us with a silver figurine of a Viking guy to remember our familial bond. The Viking guy wears a stout horned helmet on his head. His short tunic is held in place by a thick belt with a large buckle. With one arm he raises a long sword. With the other he projects a clenched fist. He has a bushy mustache that covers everything but his growling lips. He is fierce. He looks like he just yelled, "Bring it on! Bring it ALL on!"

This Viking guy greets me every morning. He reminds me to have courage. He tells me to have nerve and be bold. But the Viking guy has a problem. The problem is scale. He is brave, to be sure. But he is small. Lay him on this page and he does not quite cover six lines, from the tip of his helmet to the soles of his sandals. The Viking guy has a big heart, but he gets pushed around by coffee mugs and ballpoint pins. He is knocked over as much as he stands up. I hope he never wakes up to the fact that he is tiny. It would break his heart.

Perhaps you can relate. Does your courage ever feel undersized for the calling that you experience? We gather up our pluck and daring but find they are in short supply. When it comes to courage, we often have a problem of scale. This is especially true when our calling requires a lot of time to fulfill. We want to fulfill the words of the old hymn "Where He Leads Me":

> Where he leads me I will follow,
> where he leads me I will follow,
> where he leads me I will follow;
> I'll go with him, with him all the way.[1]

It is the "all the way" part that can be problematic. To maintain the courage that enables us to persist over time and through difficulty to accomplish what we pursue, we must fix our minds on the presence and power of Christ in us who is at work in the world today. We must take time to refocus our vision away from what is present immediately before us to what God desires to make a reality. By reminding ourselves of what we are convicted must be, we place ourselves in the presence of the kingdom of God, where discouragement, difficulty, and dilemma are all removed from view. This enables us to have hope that what we are attempting to do is worth doing.

The cycle of faith in the leadership of the Holy Spirit in our lives that offers conviction that leads to action is a paddle wheel that drives the inner working of our life in Christ, enabling us to experience courage rising in the moments it is most needed for us to do good in the world. There will be many high moments. But there will also be the constancy of commitment on our part to continue to follow the promptings of God that only courage can sustain. This will impact every part of our lives, including our ability to face hard realities, articulate our thought on important topics, and move toward people in love, especially in conversation, rather than away from them in fear.

Chapter 3

THE CANDOR OF COURAGE

One of the Pharisees asked Jesus to eat with him, and he went into the Pharisee's house and took his place at the table. And a woman in the city, who was a sinner, having learned that he was eating in the Pharisee's house, brought an alabaster jar of ointment. She stood behind him at his feet, weeping, and began to bathe his feet with her tears and to dry them with her hair. Then she continued kissing his feet and anointing them with the ointment. Now when the Pharisee who had invited him saw it, he said to himself, "If this man were a prophet, he would have known who and what kind of woman this is who is touching him—that she is a sinner." Jesus spoke up and said to him, "Simon, I have something to say to you." "Teacher," he replied, "speak." "A certain creditor had two debtors; one owed five hundred denarii, and the other fifty. When they could not pay, he canceled the debts for both of them. Now which of them will love him more?" Simon answered, "I suppose the one for whom he canceled the greater debt." And Jesus said to him, "You have judged rightly." Then turning toward the woman, he said to Simon, "Do you see this woman? I entered your house; you gave me no water for my feet, but she has bathed my feet with her tears and dried them with her hair. You gave me no kiss, but from the time I came in she has not stopped kissing my feet. You did not anoint my head with oil, but she has anointed my feet with ointment. Therefore, I tell you, her sins, which were many, have been forgiven; hence she has shown great love. But the one to whom little is forgiven, loves little." Then he said to her, "Your sins are forgiven." But those who were at the table with him began to say among themselves, "Who is this who even forgives sins?" And he said to the woman, "Your faith has saved you; go in peace."

(Luke 7:36-50)

There are few places where courage is more required than in the words we say to each other. The Bible tells us that we have to be watchful with words. Words are a powerful force in our relationships and in our society. When we speak, our words can be like small fires that set a whole forest ablaze (James 3:5). Much of conversation is just the opposite. It is mundane. The exchange of greetings, carefree banter, and shared observations between people are easy for most of us to manage. Some conversations, however, are difficult, and we may be as prone to avoid them as to undertake them.

Many years ago, a church member was so upset with me that after he forcefully shared his frustrations and concerns, he walked out of the church building promising that he would never return. I was a younger pastor at the time and realized that I did not know how to handle this moment. My first instinct was to do nothing but build a thorough rebuttal in my mind to answer the points he made to me. Perhaps you have made a similar list of things that you wish you would have said but could not articulate in that moment of conflict even if your life would have depended on it.

This man's house was visible on my daily commute from work to home and back again. My wife and I had been in that home several times for meals or meetings. I discovered twice a day, when I looked at his house, I could feel my body release a bit of adrenaline. My heart rate increased. I felt a bit of anxiety. My mind would begin to rehearse the "wish I would have said" speech.

This was not the first time such an encounter had happened. I am not a pastor who typically leads people to experience deep anger, but I would argue that if you are going do the work of a pastor, there will be times that people will be frustrated, angry, and feel the need to part from your company. When clergy in the tradition I serve are ordained, they promise to "comfort the afflicted and afflict the comfortable." It is impossible to attend to the second part of that vow without creating discomfort in others.

When I wrote the note with the four words that began with courage (see the Introduction), candor quickly followed. I realized that when I failed in verbal courage, it always had a deep impact on relationships I valued, goals we were trying to accomplish, and my sense of personal integrity. What we say and do in the midst of discomfort is a place that requires great courage. The ability to follow up with someone, attempt reconciliation, speak to injustice, or help others when they are in crisis requires us to be courageous.

I realized that I had to learn to speak in such moments. I had to learn how to speak with candor. The word *candor* may feel dated to you. It was more likely to be used in the 1800s than in the current time. Candor is the ability to be open, honest, direct, or frank in speech and conversation. When we speak with candor, we take risks. We set aside fears of whether someone might feel hurt and instead focus on how we might help the person. Candor is undergirded by honesty. It does not veer into contempt on one side or vacuous pleasantries on the other. Candor is earnest. Candor desires to state facts plainly, observe actions openly, and confront gently. Fear gets in the way of this type of conversation. Fear convinces us that if we talk about important things in life, something bad will happen. Candor is the capacity to take risks in conversation in order to help a person or organization that can only be served through an honest assessment of what is happening. In this chapter I will use *candid* as a descriptor for someone displaying candor. *Candor* is a word and skill we would be wise to resurrect.

I realized years ago that one conversation people avoided was their own death. In emergency rooms I heard families say they never talked about an advanced medical directive that would help them guide doctors on whether their loved one would want life support measures. When a person died I heard family members say they had never discussed this eventuality with their spouse or parents. When I asked why, people said, "I think it was just too uncomfortable. I was afraid to go there."

We started a new program at our church that I entitled, "Yes, You Are Going to Die." Some people did not like the title. They said that it was "just too, I don't know, too something."

"Too candid?" I offered.

"Yes!" they said.

That is when I knew I had the right title. It was essential to communicate that we were going to talk openly and honestly about something as important as death. The title did not turn people off. It brought them in. Speakers included a physician, funeral home director, attorney, and pastor. Wills were considered. Advanced medical directives were filled out, witnessed, and notarized. People sketched out their wishes, called family members or close friends and had a conversation. It took courage for people to show up. It took courage for professionals to remind people that we all die, and we do so in a variety of ways, which can be discussed. We also demonstrated that you will not die if you talk about the fact that one day you will die.

WE FAIL TO REPAIR THE HARM THAT HAPPENS IN A MOMENT SO THAT IT BECOMES A WOUND CARRIED FOR A LIFETIME.

Too often, we are not quiet and thoughtful. We are just afraid. Candor is spoken courage, and it enables us to manage difficult moments in life well. Parents need candor when they see a change in the grades, habits, and behavior of their child. Patients and doctors need candor when test results are reviewed and treatments are planned. Candor is necessary for citizens and elected officials to deal with opportunities and problems in their community. When we fail at candor, we leave important matters unresolved. We pass down problems in families from one generation to another. We pass down legacies of injustice from one century to the next. We fail to repair the harm that happens in a moment so that it becomes a wound carried for a lifetime.

JESUS WAS CANDID

Jesus demonstrates how the courage of candid dialogue enables us to create deeper relationships, change a person's view, alter the climate of a room, and encourage people around us. Jesus talked about important matters in life. Jesus was *forthright*, a word that suggests forward movement in the right direction. In order to share good news to the poor, release captives, give new vision to the blind, free the oppressed, and proclaim the Lord's favor to the least, last, and lost, he had to be able to speak directly and freely.

The dinner Jesus shared at the house of Simon the Pharisee can be seen as a small drama. Your life may feel like a small drama sometimes. If so, candor is what allows you to give voice to what is really going on with those who are present. Think of how difficult it is to resolve drama in the lives of most people. In fact, there are some who seem intent on keeping the drama alive and well for decades, like the soap opera my mother used to watch in the afternoon when I was a child. The characters were unable to resolve anything. On "As the World Turns," they kept their secrets, lied, and moved from one melodramatic episode to another. They had no "Guiding Light" that enabled them to simply get honest and real with one another. They didn't do that because if the drama ended, they would have all lost their jobs. In a similar fashion, people in families, work environments, and even churches, are sometimes invested in drama because it allows them to play a role, hold a secret, and protects them from the hard work of personal transformation or Christian sanctification.

Jesus had little interest in drama for drama's sake. He helped people move beyond drama to a candid look at their reality, so that they could choose to be made new and whole. On this night, an uninvited woman who heard Jesus would be present entered the room with a healthy dose of candor. She had lived a sinful life. Luke does not tell us what sins had been a part of her life, and there is absolutely no reason to believe that her sins were sexual in nature, but the generosity of her actions demonstrate the severity of how lost she was before she met Jesus. She wept with such intensity that she bathed Jesus's feet in her tears. She wiped her tears away with her hair and poured perfume, which is an expensive item in any era of history, on his feet. She kissed them in gratitude. Washing a person's feet at that time was a normal act of hospitality. It said, "I am a good host and you are my guest." Weeping with enough intensity to wash a rabbi's feet was an act of sustained repentance and gratitude. It is a way of telling everyone present: "I have been a sinner, my life has been broken, and this man offered me forgiveness and hope."

This woman's actions are a display of candor about her life. She is not whispering at the altar that she has been a sinner. She offers performance art. Her actions shout it to everyone at the banquet. She shows up with a frank visual statement about her life and an ardent desire for an overdue reset. In her vulnerability, she moves toward Jesus. She moves toward the experience of community with anybody who follows Jesus and resonates with the idea that "I once was lost but now am found."

Luke tells us that as Simon observes this, he says something to himself. Keeping your thoughts to yourself can be a wise way to avoid speech that you will later regret, such as a snide remark or an angry outburst. It can also be a way to avoid a candid conversation and isolate yourself from others. It can be a move away from another person or group of people due to judgment or a feeling of superiority. That is the case as Simon judges both the woman and whether Jesus was an authentic teacher and prophet. Simon thinks to himself, "If this man were a prophet, he would know who is touching him and what kind of woman she is—a sinner."

Simon's willingness to think this, but not say it out loud, is a lack of candor that is common among people. It takes courage to say things out loud.

Simon's decision not to share his thoughts is consistent with his judgment of the woman at Jesus's feet. His understanding of what it meant to live a good and righteous life in the eyes of God leads him to mentally move away from this woman. By contrast, through forgiveness, Jesus moves toward her. One sees her as a sinner. The other sees her as a child of God in need of reconciliation. Candor takes courage because it seeks to connect to its subject. Insults drive people away. Silence is a protective forcefield. Candor is a relational bid, that if accepted in response, leads people to a more intimate space of mutual honesty. Because Simon does not want to be associated with this woman, he keeps his thoughts to himself. This lack of candor allows Simon to keep his distance and also retain his sense of superiority to both the woman and Jesus.

Had Simon chosen to speak his thoughts out loud, he would not have been candid. He would have been judgmental. It is easy to confuse the two. Candor, especially for Christians, resonates with Jesus's statement that "the truth shall set you free." It is the ability to face the truth and speak of the reality that we see without fear, because God is with us, even when that reality reflects poorly on us or someone else. It is done with the intention of extending help to the relationship or to the other person in the conversation. Candor requires courage because it often must name uncomfortable facts and dynamics that people want to avoid. However, it does not name uncomfortable things in an uncomfortable fashion. When Christians are candid, they are rooted in the love of Christ that links them to kindness and compassion.

UGLINESS IS NOT CANDOR

Candor can be contrasted with the note Jimmy Curcuru, a retired Massachusetts native, received in his mailbox addressed to "Current Resident." It was anonymous, short, and cutting: "Please Paint Me! Eyesore—Your Neighbors. Thanks!"

Every pastor I know has some occasional experience with the anonymous note writer. Such people believe they are both courageous and candid. They often share complaints about sermons, perceptions about the pastor's true intentions at meetings, or offer criticisms about staff members or other congregants. These notes call people out, demand terminations, and give what the author describes as a God-inspired directive for the pastor to enact. One person, after she admitted that she drafted the anonymous note in my box, told me that she was courageous to do so. "No one else will tell you this. I simply had to do something."

I suggested that a courageous act would have been to call me, schedule an appointment, and have a conversation.

When Jimmy and his wife, Marilyn, got their note, he told reporters, "It was frustrating to read it, and it was also hurtful." The note did not give Jimmy or his wife Marilyn any new information. They were painfully aware that their home of fifty-one years was in desperate need of paint. The note did communicate judgment and leave them with a sense of shame about their situation. Their daughter Michelle posted a picture of the note on Facebook. She wanted the person who posted to see a letter her sister wrote to the anonymous author. The next day there were many supportive comments and people who offered to assist. Retailers offered discounts on renovation materials. The mayor of the town stopped by to see how she could help. One person set up a GoFundMe page to cover costs. Soon over $70,000 was contributed, the majority by people the Curcurus did not know.

Those who inquired with a desire to help did so with candor. The biggest part of candor is the willingness to knock on the door and begin a conversation. That nervous energy you feel as you knock on the door of someone you do not know to understand their situation is courage. Motivated by a desire to help, they asked questions. They learned that Jimmy had a heart attack fifteen years before that left him unable to take on major home repairs. Most of his day was spent offering care to Marilyn, who developed multiple sclerosis thirty years earlier and was now bedridden. Because people were moving toward them with interest, the Curcurus were candid in return. The worn paint was only one problem. The windows needed to be replaced along with portions of wooden siding and soffit. Inspections were done, estimates were made, and funds raised so that the work could begin.[1]

We might praise the initial note writer. Without that person, this conversation and the outpouring of help that followed would not have happened. But imagine if he or she would have cared enough to knock on the door and have a conversation rather than leaving a note that was wounding in its content and anonymity. We live in a time when if one finds a way to say whatever is on his or her mind, it is often seen as an act of courage. Jesus shows us a better way that enables us to love our neighbor with integrity.

BEGIN WITH COURTESY

When courage calls you to candor, take the first step Jesus took the night of that dinner. Jesus knows that he needs to talk about what is going on in the room. Candor begins when we realize that the moment has come when we simply must speak to another person. We must give voice to what could be easily ignored or fearfully set aside for the stir it might create. When Jesus speaks up, he begins with courtesy. Jesus, with a simple statement, seeks permission from Simon to speak: "Simon, I have something to say to you" (v. 40).

Starting well is important because it sets the tone of the entire conversation. Jesus does not make an accusation about what he sensed Simon was thinking about him or the woman who put perfume on his feet. By noting that he has something to say, Jesus makes a relational bid. He offers to move toward Simon but knows that such a movement may be rejected if Simon feels that he has no choice in the matter. When Simon replies, "Speak," he takes a step toward Jesus in the conversation. As he grants permission, he is stating his willingness to listen to what Jesus has to say.

PROCEED WITH CAUTION

The exchange is consequential in another way. By entering the conversation with permission of both parties, the conversation slows down, where everyone can do their best thinking. Jesus did not jump in the nanosecond he saw the microexpressions on Simon's face that told him of Simon's judgmental thoughts. When anger, fear, or anxiety motivates us to move too fast, we often find important conversations are derailed.

Find a Place of Agreement

When Jesus shares his parable about a creditor with two debtors, both forgiven, but for different amounts, and asks Simon's opinion as to which would be more grateful, he creates a neutral space of agreement. The parable is a math problem, and Simon correctly notes that a person forgiven much is more grateful than one forgiven of a smaller debt. There are other moments in Luke's Gospel, most notably when Jesus pronounces a series of "woes" on unrepentant cities in chapter 10 and his admonishment of religious leaders in chapter 11, when Jesus's speech is firm and direct. This typically happens when giving a speech to a large gathering of people. Jesus knows a conversation is not a speech. He does not exhort Simon.

> **WHEN WE FIND POINTS OF AGREEMENT WITH PEOPLE WITH WHOM WE DISAGREE, WE STAND IN A COMMON SPACE AS EQUALS AND PARTNERS RATHER THAN ADVERSARIES HOPING TO WIN A FIGHT.**

With this parable Jesus finds a way to gently call Simon out while still inviting him in. He gives Simon the chance to enter a dialogue about what is going on in the room where they recline at the table with other guests and observe what drives the actions of the repentant woman before them. When Simon says that the one who owed the most is the most grateful, Jesus agrees with him. When we find points of agreement with people with whom we disagree, we stand in a common space as equals and partners rather than adversaries hoping to win a fight by a higher tally of most correct points scored. It takes courage to do this, because it means that our mind might change in the process. The candor that Jesus models is one that seeks to increase understanding and change perceptions through dialogue that is rooted in respect.

Focus on the Issue

Jesus observes the events of the evening, and in doing so, takes the focus off of the woman's past and puts it on what is happening here and now. Conversation breaks down when we divert to accounts of the past rather than remaining in the present. Such diversions are a form of work avoidance. Rather than stay in the moment to resolve what is right before us, we bring up past hurts, unresolved conflicts, or observations about how one person or another is "always" this way or that. A litany of bygone events, sometimes years or decades in the past, may not even be relevant to the topic at hand; but if anxiety is high, it is easier to divert the conversation to issues and incidents that we have not reconciled or forgiven than deal with what is before us. It takes courage to do the work found in important conversations and not derail them.

Jesus shows us how to not only face the moment, but to reframe what is happening. Jesus quickly notes that the situation before them is not about the past sins of this woman, but the current lack of hospitality in Simon's home. Simon did not welcome Jesus with the customs typically offered to guests who enter your home. Simon did not offer water for Jesus's feet, greet him with a kiss, or anoint his head with oil. The woman did all these things. The simplicity and lack of condemnation in Jesus's words are what enables him to cast a spotlight on these issues without making Simon angry. They allow Jesus to invite Simon to consider the motivation of the woman who cleans the feet of his guest with tears and anoints him with expensive perfume. Rather than dwelling on the darkness of sin, Jesus lifts up the beauty of gratitude in her life that arises from her forgiveness. Either this woman has already been forgiven and comes to thank Jesus, or she is hopeful to the edge of certainty that she will be forgiven by him. Either way, her act is offered not to motivate forgiveness, but in appreciation of it.

Give People Room

Jesus does not make it personal. Jesus undoubtedly knew that nothing would make Simon feel like the walls were closing in more than his saying, "You know Simon, you are as judgmental as you are rude. That's probably why you didn't attend to the basic courtesies of hospitality! You are a terrible host!"

Perhaps you have been a part of a conversation that moved in this direction. Such outbursts lead to antagonism rather than enlightenment. Words are used to humiliate and embarrass others. Notice that Jesus does not even use Simon's name when he notes that "the one to whom little is forgiven, loves little" (v. 47).

Rather than being accusatory, candid conversations maintain the element of curiosity. They employ better questions. They invite participants to step back and examine what is taking place and consider the motivations that are at work in the lives of those involved. The dialogue enables us to consider both what each person has done and the steps each might take in the future to strengthen the relationship or to repair harm that has been done. With his simple observation about the relationship between forgiveness and love, Jesus gives Simon room to draw his own conclusions. This offers Simon the opportunity to hear the conviction of the Holy Spirit that candor encourages. Perhaps Simon will think that he is free of sin and therefore does not need forgiveness. He may also realize that there are matters in his life that could lead him to feel more grateful to God and more kind to those who enter his home. Either way, Jesus leaves Simon with the space to do his own work. Jesus does not draw conclusions for Simon or think that a stern lecture is the highway to the land of personal transformation. Jesus maintains a spirit of gentleness, a focus on the facts before them, and allows Simon to draw his own conclusions. At the same time, Jesus reframes what is before them with his observation about hospitality offered by the woman. He is able to show her as the hero who solves the crisis of poor manners rather than a sinful woman deserving of their contempt.[2] The elements of this conversation employed by Jesus do not allow animosity to take root. In this moment Jesus demonstrates how the guidelines of candor can keep us on track.

Stand with the Vulnerable

Simon is not the only party in the room. Jesus now turns his attention to the woman who has become the uncomfortable focal point of this moment. Jesus reminds her of the forgiveness that led to her act of gratitude. As he states this out loud, he again reframes what is happening in the room not only for Simon, but for the other guests. It takes courage to stand with the vulnerable person in the room. This is why people so often stick with their friends, pretend they don't notice others, or enter into judgment that eliminates the need to speak to someone.

I once asked a student how he found our church. He said that on his first day of school the year his family moved to the area, he was standing in the cafeteria wondering where to sit. A group of boys were at a table talking and laughing. One saw him standing there and called out, "Do you need a place to sit?" He said he did and was invited to join the table. He told me, "I realized that one thing these guys had in common is that they all attended Floris UMC. My parents said they wanted to find a church. When I got home I told them we should definitely come here."

When we stand with the vulnerable, or ask them to sit at our lunch table, we are acting in ways consistent with Christian discipleship. Here Jesus invites the community to see a woman they once scorned as one who has now been forgiven by God. He moves toward the woman and attempts to bring the community toward her as well. Predictably, Jesus is questioned by the other guests who ask each other where he gained the authority to forgive sins. In this way, Jesus absorbs the concerns and potential animosity of his uncomfortable fellow guests. They no longer focus their concern on the woman. They now look at Jesus this way.

No matter how well we engage in candid conversation, we should anticipate that the very act of honesty and the desire to resolve drama rather than live in it will bring criticism and the potential anger of others. Many people are unfamiliar with functional ways of dealing with the complexities of life. Courage enables us to be unbothered by those who attempt to undermine the conversation. It allows us to set our face to the wind when a person seeks damage to the reputation of the one who offers candor. Courage keeps us focused. It does not allow personal insecurity to divert us from the hard but necessary work of this restorative practice. Throughout the Gospels, Jesus shows little concern about how others view him. When he teaches, leads, and does the work of his mission, he does not take polls to chart his approval rating. His focus is to do the work of functional relationships. Jesus has no fears that limit his conversations with people. This is how he offers them the opportunity to grow in their love for God, neighbor, and themselves. Courage and candor are required elements of such discussions.

Conclude with a Blessing

We don't know what Jesus said to Simon as he left his house that evening. We do know that he turned to the woman and observed how she made good choices to begin to change her life. Jesus did not focus his parting words to her on his ability to forgive. He noted that earlier. His last words remind the woman of the goodness of what she did, along with his blessing: "Your faith has saved you; go in peace" (v. 50).

Jesus wishes her well. He invites her to fully enter a life of peace as she makes the changes they likely discussed earlier.

No matter how a conversation goes, it is helpful to conclude it with some type of blessing. Even in the worst scenarios, where a relationship is ending, it can be very helpful to simply wish a person well as they go. I have found that if someone has told me of their adamant disagreement with some view that I have expressed, if the conversation was tense or left me frustrated, it is always helpful to take a deep breath and express what I appreciate about the other person.

We must remember when reading the Gospels that we do not enjoy the perfect nature of our Lord. Since he is the Son of God, if Jesus speaks, I just assume that what he has said is correct to the point of being incisive. I don't make that assumption when I speak, even if I hold deep feelings about what I am saying. We are imperfect people who need forgiveness who speak to imperfect people who need forgiveness. Both of us may be ardent and impassioned, but that does not mean either of us got it all right. There is plenty of room for grace. If we end conversations abruptly, with ramped up feelings of anger or frustration, and then walk away, fear will creep back in and make it very difficult to pick that conversation up again in the future. When a conversation ends, the Holy Spirit will be at work in the lives of everyone who shared in the dialogue. If you find a way to conclude the conversation with a blessing, you give the Holy Spirit room to work in both your lives and open the door to the next conversation.

An easy way to end with a blessing is to learn these prompts and use them at the close of your exchange:

"Before you leave, I want to say that this has been a hard conversation and I thank you for being so honest with me."

"During this conversation you have helped me consider…"

"Here are some things that I admire about you…"

"One thing I plan to do as a result of this conversation is…"

DUAL-PURPOSE COURAGE

Courage is helpful to us in the important conversations of life in its capacity to regulate our speech. It has been long observed by great thinkers like Aristotle, Augustine, and Thomas Aquinas that courage has the dual ability to overcome fears and prevent harm. On the one hand, courage enables us to initiate conversations others would never begin. It allows us to undertake these conversations without the anxiety fear brings so that we can see them to completion. At the same time, courage enables us to understand when we are being rash in our judgments. Courage restrains us when it senses that we are about to do something that will ultimately hurt ourselves or others.

Years ago, when I was in college, I took a road trip with two others to see a fourth friend in another state. The four of us went swimming in a local river. After we made our way to the riverbank, Steve said, "Let's go up top. People jump off that railroad trestle into the water all the time. The river is deep here. I grew up doing this."

We all looked up and admired the significant distance between the river and the trestle. Steve told us to follow him. He promised that it did not look bad when you looked down on the water. We made our way out on the steel bridge and peered over. It looked pretty bad. This is where courage will help you if you allow it. One friend had a lifelong fear of heights and did not care if the rest of us knew it. He walked off immediately. The second friend stayed and began to ask questions. "What is the distance to the water? How deep is the water? What is the best way position yourself when you jump? How do we know for certain this is safe? How deep is the current level of the water?"

Courage helped him ask the right questions as he considered whether this was a wise thing to do. By contrast, I had only two words for our host. I said, "You first."

With that, Steve, whose body mass exceeded either of ours, stood on the rail and jumped. He came up from the water with a joyful shout. It took me and my second friend several minutes to do the same as we mulled over our options and watched a couple of other people take this leap of faith. Once we saw others do this safely, our own courage enabled us to take the plunge ourselves.

COURAGE ALLOWS US TO ASSESS WHEN WE MUST OVERCOME OUR FEARS AND ACT, AND WHEN AN ACTION IS IRRESPONSIBLE AND MAY CAUSE LASTING HARM TO US OR THE LIVES OF OTHERS.

The point is that not every jump is safe or wise. God works for good in our lives. God wants to offer us the ability to fulfill the deep longing of our calling and grow deeper in our sanctification. Courage is the virtue God uses to consider and regulate risk. Courage allows us to assess when we must overcome our fears and act, and when an action is irresponsible and may cause lasting harm to us or the lives of others. Many think the courageous person will jump off every height any time someone dares her or him to do it. Courage, in such an instance, has been confused with bravado and swagger.

REMEMBER THE GOAL

In conversation, there are times we must take the plunge, even if the thought of talking to a certain person about a certain topic is daunting to us. There are also moments when we are wise to wait for a more opportune moment to initiate conversation. Courage calls us to use our minds to consider and weigh our options. It calls us to use our hearts as we seek the counsel of God in prayer. God uses this virtue to keep us from the harm that inevitably comes when we rush into a conversation with nothing more than a bundle of partially formed opinions along with a couple of loose accusations.

Our goal is to be more like Jesus and less like the person who speaks in ways that consistently harm others with his or her words. If you follow Jesus, you enter a life of love that is demonstrated in decency and kindness. Some Christians feel disoriented in the current time because the culture of speech has veered away from civil discourse and encouraged audacious and unkind statements toward others, a valid, if not encouraged, form of self-expression. Decency and kindness are hallmarks of Christian speech and conversation. This relates to courage, because it is the virtue that calls out all the rest of our virtues, like wisdom, restraint, and fairness. Courage calls us to hold these standards in our speech even when the culture around us seems to have lost these values.

It doesn't really bother me when people who have no faith in God are unkind when they speak. Such people may not hold kindness as a personal value. What is troubling is when we hear people who call themselves "Christian" say and do things that are consistently unpleasant, hostile, or cruel. To be kind is a basic expression of our relationship with Christ. It demonstrates that the light and love of Christ have entered our nature. When we know Jesus, his love is reflected in our words, our actions, and our ability, when someone else is hotheaded, not to throw fuel on their flame but to be a person of peace. All this and more is kindness.

Never has kindness in speech been so important. Our children have many negative role models. Some, who loudly proclaim themselves as Christians, or lead institutions that are supposedly based on the Christian faith, seem to revel in audacious statements in the news or social media that are simply unkind.

As Jesus once said as he discussed the nature of true greatness with his disciples, "It will not be so among you" (Matthew 20:26).

When we ask God to give us courage in necessary conversations, the gift is not just the ability to do the work. Courage enables the candor to do the work well, because it brings with it wisdom and the desire to show love to another person. Then it enables us to speak with a desire to bring blessing instead of harm, and reconciliation rather than wrath. Such conversations lead people and organizations forward. The virtue of courage enables the expression of our Christian discipleship in our words and actions. This can be difficult, even as we gain skills to resolve conflict and carefully consider how to conduct ourselves.

Conversations bring pressure. Relationships can be strained to the breaking point. The stakes are high. In order to do this consistently, with people as important as our family members, friends, coworkers, and neighbors in the world, we have to maintain our courage and a desire to show love in the words we share.

Chapter 4
THE HOPE
OF COURAGE

One day, while [Jesus] was teaching, Pharisees and teachers of the law were sitting near by (they had come from every village of Galilee and Judea and from Jerusalem); and the power of the Lord was with him to heal. Just then some men came, carrying a paralyzed man on a bed. They were trying to bring him in and lay him before Jesus; but finding no way to bring him in because of the crowd, they went up on the roof and let him down with his bed through the tiles into the middle of the crowd in front of Jesus.

(Luke 5:17-19)

There are times when the best thing our friends can do is help us make an appointment for a good "come to Jesus meeting." When I hear that term, it is rarely positive. It typically describes a strong discussion that exceeds the boundaries of kindness described in the last chapter. But there is another kind of meeting, one where we come to Jesus because he is the only hope we have left.

The man who suffered paralysis had a lot going on in his life. Many in that time assumed that if you were sick or had a disability, it was a sign that you had committed a great sin. Such a view indicates that the one who holds it sees life through a lens of retributive justice. God becomes the Punisher-In-Chief, separating the naughty and nice by harming those who are on the bad list. It would be pretty easy to lose hope in the goodness of God or the possibility of healing if you held such a view, even if you did not embrace it initially. The longer the illness or disability lasted, the easier it would be to assume the beliefs of those who believed that God wanted to penalize rather than help you. After years of trying to get better, this man may have no longer been on speaking terms with courage, even as it told him to try again. He may have just given up.

WHAT IS HOPE?

On my desk there is a note with one word. It reads "...yet." I was feeling defeated one day and wrote that note to remind myself that I did not have to be disappointed that a goal had not been achieved. I needed to understand that the goal had simply not been achieved yet. We give up sometimes. Expectations are not met. Confidence in the future is lost. Even courage, which so often comes at just the right moment, no longer inspires us. Once exciting chapters of our lives end in misfortune, or even tragedy, and we let go of the thought that things will get better. That is why courage requires hope. Hope is the assurance that God is faithful and that the purposes God has called you to undertake will be completed. Hope is the capacity to carry the expectation of the fulfillment of a task while working diligently and waiting patiently for an outcome that is in keeping with God's goodness, righteousness, and justice.

Courage without hope is like a sail without wind. Hope, in the Christian life, has an importance of biblical proportions. Hope is the knowledge that goodness and mercy will follow us all the days of our lives and we shall dwell in the house of the Lord forever. It is the certainty that the kingdom of God is at hand. Hope is the courage that refuses to doubt God's goodness even when a cause to which a person is committed is not being accomplished in the way she or he hoped or at the speed the person desires. Hope is what Jesus spoke to when he promised, "And remember, I am with you always, to the end of the age" (Matthew 28:20).

A LITTLE HELP FROM MY FRIENDS

When we lose hope, it is wise to cling to good friends and others who care. Friends are the means of grace God uses to carry us through difficult times. Friends believe for us when we cannot find a way to believe for ourselves.

One of the greatest examples of a large group of people who held on to hope together when they had every right to give up is those who used the "Lost Friends" column in the *Southwestern Christian Advocate*. This was a Methodist newspaper that went out to nearly five hundred preachers, eight hundred post offices, and more than four thousand subscription holders from the end of Reconstruction to the beginning of the Jim Crow era. The advertisement placed there by Si Johnson in 1881 is a good example of ads run by formerly enslaved people who wanted to find their lost family members. Mr. Johnson was separated from his parents forty-seven years earlier when the estate of the man who enslaved his family was divided.

> I desire to find my parents.... My mother said, the morning she was going to leave, "My son you must be a good child." I was standing in my father's house by a little table near the door, he said to me, "My son you are five years old to-day." It was in 1834. Miss Lureasy Cuff was standing in the house and talking to my mother, and saying, "I think pa should give Si to me, because I raised him to what he is." Uncle Thomas drove the wagon when mother left.[1]

Millions of formerly enslaved persons were separated from their wives, husbands, parents, and children. They were broken up and spread abroad by the churning waters of chattel slavery, where the loving bond of family was sacrificed on the altar of economic gain. Undoubtedly many lost the hope that they would ever find family members after the time of emancipation. The brutality of enslavement, combined with the system's lack of record keeping, enforced illiteracy, and endemic poverty made a true search for lost loved ones nearly impossible. These ads were testimony to the hope that lived in some, often nurtured by their trust that with God, all things are possible. The ads were read from pulpits each Sunday so that anyone with information might assist those searching for their family members.

Reading through the heartfelt words of the advertisements in the Lost Friends database is a moving experience. The longing expressed to find family members and loved ones is poignant. These ads required people who were likely to be very poor to invest their money in the hope of locating the people they loved. It is a remarkable example of the way people can work together to keep hope alive. The preachers who read the ads from the pulpit did so with the hope that someone might just know this person or recall that name. The subscribers who shared the ads with their neighbors did so with the hope that they might help persons find someone important that they lost years earlier. As the ads were read and shared, people held hope for one another. They believed for each other. This long strand of individuals and congregations, spanning multiple southern states, connected the person who took out the ad on one end to the loved one described in the ad at the other. In some cases, lost family members and friends were reunited. What a day that must have been for those involved to learn that the fruit of their hope was the restoration of once-vanished family members.

We need others to sustain the hope that reinvigorates our own courage. I wonder whose idea it was to bring the man with paralysis to meet Jesus. It could have been the man himself. But I think it was probably the friends. Imagine that the friends hear that Jesus is in the area. If Jesus has healed others, he can heal their friend. Imagine the man yelling, "What are you doing?!" as they pick up the bed he lies on and carry him out the door. These men are problem solvers. When they arrive, they see that there is a big crowd around the house where Jesus is teaching. They will never get their friend inside through the normal route. I picture them going to the back of the house. One by one they get on the roof and drag ropes up behind them as they carefully lift their friend. They begin digging through the thatch style roof until dust is falling on the people inside. Suddenly a new skylight has been created. Everyone inside begins to move out of the way as this man, still lying on his bed but now holding on for dear life, slowly descends. It's like the big moment in a Broadway show.

Here is what the friends know: when hope is lost, it is time to find Jesus.

WHEN HOPE IS LOST, IT IS TIME TO FIND JESUS.

HOPE CAN BE HARD

Before he was born, angels promised that Jesus was Emmanuel, "God is with us" (Matthew 1:23).

We need hope in God's presence with us because our courage tank can be drained over time. There are two reasons for this. First, life will test you. Life can be wondrous. Life can be beautiful. Life can be rich with meaning. But one thing is for certain: life will be difficult. And when we come to the difficult parts, we learn why "you can do hard things" is a well-known mantra.

Sometimes things happen in life that are so hard that you measure your life as the time before the terrible event and the time after. I have a friend in Washington, D.C., who went through something like that. On a very normal night several years ago, her life was abruptly altered.

The police were called around 4:30 a.m. by her neighbor. She had been attacked by an intruder in her home. Somehow, she made it out of the house. In that terrible moment, small acts of kindness began. A neighbor covered her with a blanket.

She suffered a traumatic brain injury and spent months recovering. Family and friends came to the hospital. Like the friends of the man who was paralyzed, she was surrounded by the concern and love of others. Their love was dependable, but it could only be a small part of her healing. The trauma of such an event is life-altering. It creates a downward spiral. Normally at peace in the routines of her life, she was now terrified. In the year that followed, she quit her job and sequestered herself in her apartment. She knew that something had to change.

She allowed courage to move her forward. She started over. She moved to a new city. She got a new job. She invested in herself. She learned to live free of fear. She made herself vulnerable, a remarkably courageous act for someone whose life and body were so violated. She shared her story to help and encourage other victims of sexual violence. In so doing, she offered insights that helped people who experience trauma and suffering in other forms. Few people know more about the volume of courage necessary to embrace life again than those who have suffered trauma and then live and believe in such a way as to restore hope in their life. When I hear a story like this, I am reminded that a great and loving God is willing to journey with us through the valley of the shadow of death, so that we have hope of emerging on the other side.

The second reason we need hope is that while life in general is difficult, the Christian life is no walk in the park either. When you accept Jesus as your Lord and Savior and ask him to both sanctify you in love and put you to work in the world, your life does not become all daisies and roses. The narrow path is not Easy Street. Christian discipleship means personal transformation, and if there is one thing human beings often find challenging, it is change. Jesus does not call people to easy things. He calls us to tasks that we can only accomplish if he is present to guide us, empower us, and even do a miracle or two along the way to remind us that all day long God is working for good in the world.

WHY DO WE NEED HOPE?

Courage is essential to the Christian life, but it must be yoked to hope in the power of God in our lives. Courage wakes us up every morning, yells "Rise and shine," and tells us to get dressed and get to work. Yet courage fades. Courage needs hope to serve coffee in the late afternoon, when the work is not done but we feel that quitting time has come. Hope reminds us that with God's help, we can do the things God asks us to do.

Hope enables us to persist and persevere in the Christian life over years and decades of time. This is necessary because you never know where faithful discipleship in Christ will lead. There could be conflict with family, the loss of a friend, the need to take a stand on an important moral issue, or the requirement to give up on a habit or pursuit that is clearly beyond the gracious boundaries the Lord has laid out for us. These are just some of the items that Jesus said came with the decision to follow him.

Courage is needed in the love God calls us to offer others. Such love can diminish when it is rejected. It can fade, especially when those we love make bad or sometimes tragic decisions. It can be overwhelmed when evil things happen to them and situations become too complex for us. This is when relational courage is tested.

While writing this manuscript I received a message from my daughter, Kathryn. She is a special education teacher in a public school whose students often come from cash-poor neighborhoods. She loves her vocation and works hard to build relationships with students that promote learning. A history of racial inequity in the city where she works, fueled by a longstanding lack of funding and investment aimed at the neighborhoods, school, and institutions her students pass through, is linked to higher rates of violence linked to poverty. She shared that a student she greatly enjoyed when she taught in another city two years ago was hospitalized after being shot several times while his younger siblings looked on. This young man's parent called Ms. Berlin because she knew all the time and energy she had invested in her child. She knew she cared. Kathryn was able to call this student and communicate her concern for him. The two were able to laugh over happy memories on the phone even while he was lying in his hospital bed.

After Kathryn shared all of this, I began to think of all the parents, teachers, coaches, and neighbors who invest countless hours in children who live in places where violence is a symptom of poverty and where a student can be wounded or die quickly. There are also students who live in more privileged places but who suffer for other reasons. Emotional health can be fragile. Drug use can turn to drug addiction and overdose. Every year communities lose teenagers who take their own life in despair.

Hope keeps teachers teaching. It enables parents to continue to invest in their children. It leads community organizers and politicians to focus on areas where children are at risk because they have opportunities to make a difference. Hope empowers the most persistent acts of love in your life because it tells you that the people you care for in difficult situations are not lost causes. Your child is not a lost cause. Your student, parishioner, customer, coworker, or patient is not a lost cause. The man who is homeless that you pass going into the library is not a lost cause. Hope reminds us that these are children of God, even in moments when they don't seem to know that or act in keeping with that identity. Hope whispers that the good you strive to see fulfilled will come to life by the grace of God, maybe soon, maybe later, maybe not in the time of your particular life. It tells you to take courage and keep after it anyway. In so doing, hope enables courage to rise again. This can be the difference in getting up every day having given up a long time ago and getting up to face the day, knowing that you have important work to accomplish.

GOD IS FOR US

The apostle Paul said that God is at work in the hard parts of our lives, when we need courage the most. He stated the importance of hope and its connection to the love of God in his Letter to the Romans:

> Not only that, but we also boast in our sufferings, knowing that suffering produces endurance, and endurance produces character, and character produces hope, and hope does not disappoint us, because God's love has been poured into our hearts through the Holy Spirit that has been given to us.
> (Romans 5:3-5)

Hope is the product of endurance, but it is also the glimmer of light that motivates us to endure. We must endure in life. We must persevere. Perseverance is courage pressed down and rolled out. Courage, to be sustained before it is spread too thin, needs hope to reconstitute and reinvigorate it. Paul says that it is possible because God's love has been poured into our hearts. It is helpful for Paul to remind us that as we deal with the disappointments and difficulties of life, God is not only with us, but God is also for us.

The first months of the global COVID-19 pandemic were a difficult time. People were very concerned about their health and the impact of catching the virus. Everyone had to make radical changes in life. Every institution of society and commerce had to change the way it did business to continue to operate. Fear was prevalent. Fear of sickness. Fear of death. Fear of job loss. Fear of failure. Anxiety was high for everyone. On Sunday morning I was in my backyard. I felt out of sorts as a pastor, who, having prerecorded our worship service, was free on a Sunday morning. I felt that I no longer knew how to do my job. I was concerned for my church members and for the church itself. I had done my best to appear confident and hopeful, but in truth, I was feeling some despair.

One morning, a nervous glance at my phone revealed that an English friend had sent an email with a link marked, "UK Blessing." It was a link to a YouTube video. Musicians from churches recorded themselves singing "The Blessing" in their homes. Some video genius brought them together as a compilation, with each singer in their own window, and, in one video, enabled them to sing as a virtual choir. The text of the song was based on Numbers 6:24-26, which begins, "The Lord bless you and keep you."

As it played on my phone screen through earphones, I found it to be a powerful song. As it concluded, I was deeply moved. I found myself in tears. I was shocked at such a deep emotional response in such a short period of time. When the song finished, I wiped a tear from my cheek and said, "Where did that come from!!??"

It was sometime later that I understood what happened. I listened again, carefully. It ends with a refrain that underscores this truth: God is for you. The singers repeat that truth no less than ten times.

I had convinced myself that I was on my own, that the safety of my family and the weight and worry of my work were somehow all on my shoulders. That day, my courage seemed exhausted. I questioned if I would persevere. The song reminded me of something very simple: God is for you. I realized that I was not alone. I felt that if such a beautiful thing was possible—even in the midst of, or perhaps even because of the pandemic—other things must be possible as well.

It gave me hope, and hope, as Paul says, does not disappoint us. Hope renews the courage needed to continue to do what God calls us to do.

HOPE RENEWS THE COURAGE NEEDED TO CONTINUE TO DO WHAT GOD CALLS US TO DO.

I wonder, when the man with paralysis was lowered through the roof, was he fearful, or laughing with delight at the extreme measures his friends used to put him in front of Jesus? We don't know the cause of his difficulty. Only Jesus knew what needed to be healed in his life. Like most people, I would guess that he had health that needed to be restored and sin that needed to be forgiven. Perhaps that is why Jesus makes two statements instead of one:

> "Friend, your sins are forgiven you."
> (Luke 5:20)

> "So that you may know that the Son of Man has authority on earth to forgive sins"—he said to the one who was paralyzed—"I say to you, stand up and take your bed and go to your home."
> (Luke 5:24)

When hope is restored, we can take the next faithful steps in life.

HOW DO WE SUSTAIN HOPE?

If you and I want to sustain hope, we have to stay connected to Christ. The Gospel of John offers a very confident view of the power of Christ to overcome the hardships and suffering of the world. Jesus said, "I am the light of the world. Whoever follows me will never walk in darkness but will have the light of life" (John 8:12).

Many interpret the darkness referenced here as the darkness of sin. But what if the healing we need is not just about a moral failure or a decision to forsake God? Darkness here might include the sense of dreariness and despair that comes when we lose hope. In such moments, our once-vigorous courage becomes an atrophied muscle that is of little help. John calls us to focus on the light of Christ rather than our own. We no longer have to conjure up our own courage or the hope that underlies it. The light of Christ is so sufficient and so dependable we can trust it fully. This theme is also found in the Revelation to John, where light is the central image in the vision of the Holy City, the New Jerusalem. John writes, "The city has no need of the sun or moon to shine on it, for the glory of God is its light, and its lamp is the Lamb. The nations will walk by its light, and the kings of the earth will bring their glory into it. Its gates will never be shut by day—and there will be no night there" (Revelation 21:23-25).

Here the glory of God is said to be so great that the light of the sun is just not necessary. If we need light, we need to think of ourselves as solar panels, seeking the light of Christ to enable us to burn brightly. The problem is that we often endure dark days and even seasons when the light does not get through. Clouds form, rain falls. While our panels may be turned in the right direction, it feels like the light is not getting through in ways sufficient to restore hope and confidence. Despair is not the recognition that life is hard. It is the belief that there will not be sufficient help to lift us out of times of hardship. It is the conclusion that change is no longer possible. In such a time, life is no longer lived. It is endured. Worse yet, it is ended.

John understands this dynamic in our lives and speaks to it early in his Gospel. In the first chapter he writes, "The light shines in the darkness, and the darkness did not overcome it" (John 1:5).

That is important to remember when you feel like the darkness is absolutely overcoming you. Hope, the knowledge that God is for us and with us and will ultimately be victorious, is the light that God puts in the life of one who lives as a disciple of Jesus Christ. Jesus said that when we became his disciples, we took his light into our lives. His light is ultimately what fuels the love we show others and the hope that we maintain. Jesus tells us that we must look within to see if his light is overcoming the darkness we experience.

> "No one after lighting a lamp puts it in a cellar, but on the lampstand so that those who enter may see the light. Your eye is the lamp of your body. If your eye is healthy, your whole body is full of light; but if it is not healthy, your body is full of darkness. Therefore consider whether the light in you is not darkness. If then your whole body is full of light, with no part of it in darkness, it will be as full of light as when a lamp gives you light with its rays."
>
> (Luke 11:33-36)

Jesus tells us that we must look within to see if the light of Christ is present. Hope arises out of the ongoing relationship that we have with Christ. The radiant presence of Christ within our lives is the light others observe when we do the work of our calling. We must evaluate whether Christ is still present when we look within. It is easy to become so busy with the work courage inspires that we forget to attend to the relationship with Christ that sustains our hope over time. Once that flame has burned out, Jesus tells us that it will be dark indeed. If the flame is low, then something must be done to rekindle it before darkness overcomes the light that Christ intends in our lives. It takes more than a one-time decision to maintain the light of Christ. Intentionality is required of those who want to keep the flame of the lamp alive.

Visitors to Arlington National Cemetery often stop at the gravesite of President John F. Kennedy. The site is known for the eternal flame, a feature that First Lady Jacqueline Kennedy requested for her husband's grave. Thousands of people visit this site annually and find the eternal flame burning brightly in all kinds of weather. "Eternal flame" certainly sounds dependable, and for the most part it is. But there have been moments when it was extinguished. One occurred only a month after the flame was hurriedly installed for President Kennedy's funeral. A group of children from a Catholic school came to pay their respects to the fallen President. They were taking turns sprinkling holy water on the grave when the cap came off the bottle and a stream of water fell directly on the flame, extinguishing it.[2]

One can only imagine the reaction of the school chaperones who accompanied the group as they overcame their initial astonishment and began a mad scramble to find a way to restart the flame. I think of those children and the memory they carried of that event as they grew up. Somewhere there is an adult who knows, deep in her or his heart, that she or he is the person who doused the eternal flame. I imagine that person wincing as he or she thinks of it every time he or she strikes a match, lights a gas grill, or pours water from a bottle. The good news is that the flame was quickly relit by a nearby worker, but it demonstrated that the eternal flame was fragile. When a permanent memorial was created, a new eternal flame was installed. Over the years the gas tanks, igniter, and fuel lines that create the eternal flame have been adjusted, replaced, and upgraded. Whenever this work is done, a temporary flame is kept lit nearby to honor President Kennedy. The work performed on this system through the years reveals that no flame is actually eternal. When courage inspires us to undertake some action or engage some relationship as an act of love in the world, we learn that we have to be intentional about maintaining the flame. When people do good things in the world, circumstances or the actions of people who feel that they might lose something if that good is accomplished combine to shower our flame. Keeping the radiance of Christ alive in your soul is worth the investment. In the end, it is our knowledge of God's presence that keeps hope alive.

IT IS OUR KNOWLEDGE OF GOD'S PRESENCE THAT KEEPS HOPE ALIVE.

CULTIVATING HOPE

Rest

Courage can wear you out if you are not careful. This is what you never think of when you first catch the clear glimpse of the good God calls you to do. You can see the goal. You can sketch out a path between where you are and where you must go if that is to be accomplished. Then the obstacles come. Then the controversy breaks out. The money runs low and the supporters walk away. Soon a vision that was burning in your bones becomes the cause of a bad case of indigestion. You lose sleep. You feel stressed out, worn down, and are ready to cash out. It sounds odd to say that if persons want to sustain hope, they need to disengage and experience a period of recovery. Daily this is done through proper sleep and exercise. Regularly it is wise to pull away, as Jesus did, from the crowds and demands of life. Rest has the capacity to restore us.

Read the Bible

I have read the Bible a lot over the years. Even though I know the story, I need to be reminded of it regularly. When I read the Bible, I renew my relationship with God, the person of Christ, and the presence of the Holy Spirit. I am amazed how a chapter of the Bible can give me wisdom I need for that particular day and how it can calm my spirit. I have found that using an audio version of the Bible helps me connect to the Bible in a fresh way. No matter how I experience it, I am reminded that God is with me.

Surround Yourself with Wise People

Listen to people who have wisdom about the Christian faith. Get in a group with them. Develop a friendship. Interview them. Let them talk about why their marriage is so good, how they dealt with their health crisis, how they raised their children, and how they did so well in their vocation. Listen for people who have joy in life because they have a friendship with God. They are a gift, like the girl in math class who would let you come over after school and explained calculus in ways that made sense. They give hope because they offer wisdom about how faith in Christ brings goodness to your life.

Connect with People of Peace

As Jesus sends out seventy of his disciples to do the work of the reign of God, he instructs them, "If anyone is there who shares in peace, your peace will rest on that person; but if not, it will return to you" (Luke 10:6).

Jesus tells them to find the people of peace in the village. People of peace are those who extend a welcome to you. They show you hospitality. They are the people who invite you in because they know how to connect to others. Such people restore hope because they are easy to be with. They fill you up rather than sucking you dry.

Practice Silence and Christian Meditation

Jesus demonstrated the power of silence and prayer. In Scripture, God commands us to "be still, and know that I am God!" (Psalm 46:10). If we want the Holy Spirit to open the streams that fill our hope reservoirs, we are wise to attend to the practice of silence that is focused on the holy. Gain spaces and practices that wall off anxiety and allow you to be at peace.

Search for Beauty

Walk a dog, hike in the woods, play with a child, admire someone's ability or work, sit on the beach, go to a museum, listen to a concert, attend the performance of a dance company, enjoy a sunrise, and then go watch the sunset. Do things that help you take in the beauty God has made, which is both in nature and in the beauty that humans produce in so many varied ways. I once arrived an hour early for a meeting in Washington, D.C. As I approached the National Gallery of Art, a parking place magically opened up. I pulled in, went inside, and took in works of the Impressionists in paint and sculpture for forty minutes. I was amazed how being in the presence of beautiful things renewed my spirit by the time I arrived at my meeting.

Claim Your "Ebenezers"

The prophet Samuel gives us a hopeful practice when he "took a stone and set it up between Mizpah and Jeshanah, and named it Ebenezer; for he said, 'Thus far the LORD has helped us'" (1 Samuel 7:12). It is important to find ways to mark occasions and remember the times in life that the Lord helped us. It may be a stone, but it could be a photo album or a joyful conversation where you reminisce with a friend. When we find ways to remember how the Lord has helped us, we foreshadow the good God will continue to do in our lives in the future. We realize that just as our life has endured hardship, it also contains miraculous moments of goodness. The hymn writer testifies, "Here I raise my Ebenezer"[3] as a suggestion to the rest of us to remember that if God was with you in the past, then God is with you today. From such knowledge hope is renewed.

Chapter 5

THE FORTITUDE OF COURAGE

Jesus called the twelve together and gave them power and authority over all demons and to cure diseases, and he sent them out to proclaim the kingdom of God and to heal. He said to them, "Take nothing for your journey, no staff, nor bag, nor bread, nor money—not even an extra tunic. Whatever house you enter, stay there, and leave from there. Wherever they do not welcome you, as you are leaving that town shake the dust off your feet as a testimony against them." They departed and went through the villages, bringing the good news and curing diseases everywhere.

(Luke 9:1-6)

Fortitude is courage that has the potency to endure, especially in times of adversity. No matter what mission you pursue, whether raising a child, sharing your faith in Christ, or working on some issue of justice in your community, you have to put yourself out there. You will feel exposed, especially when things go wrong. Vulnerability is a part of this. Jesus intentionally makes his disciples experience what it is like to feel exposed from the moment he tells them to go out into their community. Perhaps he does it to improve their prayer life. He wants them to get to the end of their personal reserves quickly so that they feel the need to turn to God for their most basic of needs.

Fortitude comes when we draw our strength from God rather than our limited reservoir. When we learn to tap into God's power, courage becomes Christian fortitude, the strength to endure.

A CHICK IN FEBRUARY

My friend Walter had a small horse farm not far from where I live. Along with some horses, he kept a couple of turkeys and some peacocks. When our daughters were young, they loved going out there to ride the horses and chase the birds. Walter decided to get some chickens for the farm. He ordered the eggs through the mail, set up an incubator in his barn, and was excited when they all hatched. He had twenty-five little chicks. Then he was called out of town for an unexpected business trip. He was single, and it was February and very cold. So, he called his good old cousin Tom to see if the girls wanted to keep some chicks for a week.

When Walter dropped off the chicks, they were still in the incubator. He showed me the warming bar in the metal cage that housed the chicks. It had a high-wattage light attached to it. All the chicks were gathered under that bar, peeping their little heads off. Those chicks never went far from that heat bar. They might run into the next compartment to get some feed or water for a moment. In a flash they were pushing their way back to the bar. As we looked at those chicks, I could see why they were so cold. They were scrawny. They had just a few tiny little feathers. There was little to keep them warm.

Walter said, "If the light goes out, it means the heat bar is no longer working."

I said, "Then what do I do?"

He pulled a lamp with an oversized bulb out of a box he was carrying. "You plug this in and place it on top of the cage like this. Make sure it stays on or the chicks will freeze to death."

"What else is in the box?" I asked.

"Another heat lamp in case this one breaks."

"Isn't that overkill?" I asked.

"Not if you are a chick in February," he observed.

All week long those scrawny little chicks stuck close to the heat bar. We checked on them several times a day. I was pleased to tell Walter when he returned that we only lost one chick that week. When it died, the chick was as far away from the heat bar as it could get.

Going it alone often seems like a great idea. After all, you get more space for yourself. The difficulty is that we grow cold fast. We learn that the real strength in our lives is not self-manufactured. Our strength draws from the glory of God, the love of Christ, and the power of the Holy Spirit. Our desire to connect to God, however, is a reflection of another truth. We are made for community with others. Our courage seeks the courage of others so that it can be reinforced. This is how we are encouraged. Other people put their courage into us. They revive us. Discouragement is the experience of waning fortitude common to us all. Other people strengthen us by example and through their words of encouragement. The chickens are not just looking for heat. They instinctually know that they are better together.

Jesus spoke about this while standing on a hill overlooking Jerusalem. He could see the city and its inhabitants. He said,

> "Jerusalem, Jerusalem, the city that kills the prophets and stones those who are sent to it! How often have I desired to gather your children together as a hen gathers her brood under her wings, and you were not willing!"
>
> (Luke 13:34)

He is speaking a prophetic word about the fickle nature of human beings. We say we want a message from God, but then get angry at those who deliver it. He knows he will be killed by them as well. As he says this, Jesus uses an image that captures both the strength we find when we are drawn to God and, at the same time, enter closer community with others. Jesus describes God as a mother hen who creates a space of security where we are drawn closer to others. In so doing, we find the ability to endure. We find a strength that is not our own, but which becomes the source of our fortitude.

The strength of fortitude is uniquely the property of those who actively gather together under the protective wings of God. When we depend only on the personal confidence that courses through our veins, courage begins to fail. Soon we discover that we can all be that little chicken. Compared to the challenge we are undertaking, we are scrawny. We don't have enough feathers to keep courage warm and vital. Prayer and trust in Christ are the ways Jesus's followers keep themselves near the heat and light of God's presence where fortitude thrives. Our trust in Christ must be overt. It is a confession that we make. We have to say it out loud before it is actualized in our lives. Peter was the first disciple to experience the power of stating his understanding of Jesus's identity.

OUR WHOLE HEARTS

One day when Jesus was praying alone, with only the disciples near him, he asked them, "Who do the crowds say that I am?" They answered, "John the Baptist; but others, Elijah; and still others, that one of the ancient prophets has arisen."

(Luke 9:18-19)

Then Jesus narrowed the focus. "But who do you say I am?" It is a powerful question because the man who responds has to expose himself to risk. It is a vulnerable place to stand. The response requires the man to define his relationship with Jesus. There is an emotional exposure regarding what Jesus or the other men around him will think of this important answer.

When Peter replies, "The Messiah of God," he elevates the risk by turning the answer into a pass-or-fail moment. You cannot "sort of" be the Messiah of God. You either are the Messiah of God, or you are not. The statistical likelihood of being the Messiah of God is infinitely small, so putting that label on the right person is a big gamble. In his belief in Jesus, Peter is all in. Peter is wholehearted. Matthew tells us of Jesus's excitement when he heard Peter's response:

"Blessed are you, Simon son of Jonah! For flesh and blood has not revealed this to you, but my Father in heaven. And I tell you, you are Peter, and on this

rock I will build my church, and the gates of Hades
will not prevail against it."

(Matthew 16:17-18)

In such moments, fortitude is born. Peter has pushed all his chips to the center of the table. He is betting everything he has on Jesus.

On a podcast, I once heard author and social scientist Brené Brown say she calls people who are "all in" about life, who live and love entirely, "wholehearted." Her source for that term was the *Book of Common Prayer* of the Episcopal Church.[1] The liturgy of Holy Communion, used in many Christian traditions, states, "Merciful God, we confess that we have not loved you with our whole hearts."

Brown stated that people are vulnerable in three ways: uncertainty, risk, and emotional exposure. Wholehearted people are willing to endure these key areas of vulnerability in order to love people, accomplish goals, and pursue dreams. People who are not wholehearted live lesser lives because they are much more likely to succumb to their fears or live in constant response to perceptions of how others see them.

COURAGE IS DEPENDENT ON THE COMMITMENT OF OUR HEART TOWARD THE OBJECT OF OUR ATTENTION.

Jesus calls all of us to be as wholehearted as Peter. Peter demonstrates that wholeheartedness is the beginning of courage. It has long been recognized that courage is dependent on the commitment of our heart toward the object of our attention. The word *courage* comes from the Old French *corage*, which meant "heart," "innermost feelings." or "temper."[2] His conviction that Jesus is the Messiah of God is what will lead him to be one of the most courageous disciples who ever lived. In Acts, we see Peter do miracles, teach crowds, and lead people to faith in Christ that transforms their lives. Peter is wholehearted in his conviction about Jesus's identity and power, and his courage emanates from it.

Conviction about Christ is the shield fortitude carries into battle. When it is lacking, we are tempted to desert our posts or surrender. Peter's life, like our own, was not fully consistent. Peter denied Christ three times at the time of Jesus's arrest and trial before abandoning him as the other disciples had done earlier. This is an example of what fear can do in our hearts. Fear convinces us that we are alone and cannot handle the pressure of what God has asked us to do. It tells us to abandon our calling and save ourselves. Our brains are uniquely wired to motivate us to fight, flee, or freeze when we experience fear. When we are wholehearted, we override the primal urge of self-preservation and honor our intention to serve other people or a broader community. Fortitude can only exist in such an environment.

One Sunday I shared in a sermon that I was struggling to maintain hope about work I was doing with others in our denomination. Floris United Methodist Church, where I serve, had undergone a time of self-definition. We developed a logo that expressed our desire to be "1Church4All," to say out loud that we wanted to intentionally welcome and include people of all races, all abilities, and all sexual orientations and identities in our congregation. It required a great deal of time and effort on the part of many in our congregation to express those ideas openly and with enthusiasm. Helping The United Methodist Church do the same through its global General Conference was far more difficult and success appeared less likely. The following week a couple in our church came by my office with a gift bag. They were excited to share it with me. I looked under the tissue paper inside and found a wooden plaque that read, "Let Your Faith Be Bigger Than Your Fear."

As I held the plaque, they said, "We are so grateful to go to a church that welcomes us and our friends in this community. We are proud to be a part of this congregation and we know this is not easy work. Please don't give up. We hope this plaque will remind you that we are in this together, and we should not be afraid."

On the back of the plaque they wrote, "Tom, stay strong!"

That was their way of telling me to have courage, to exhibit fortitude in a calling to see the church be a truly welcoming community, for the love of Christ to be extended to everyone. Christian fortitude is uniquely available to those who follow Peter in his confession of Jesus as the Christ and then attempt to live as a disciple who hears God's calling and acts upon it.

The strength to endure hardship and difficulty is required in our personal lives. It is also required of churches and organizations. They must be wholehearted as well, or risk the regrets that fear brings to our life together. When we are not wholehearted, we lack the fortitude to uphold the integrity of our deepest beliefs. We surrender our values to perceived necessities of the age in which we live. History belongs to those principled people, churches, and organizations with the fortitude to consistently endure as they followed the command of Christ:

> "You shall love the Lord your God with all your heart, and with all your soul, and with all your strength, and with all your mind; and your neighbor as yourself."
> (Luke 10:27)

John Wesley, the founder of Methodism, found the enslavement of African men, women, and children to be horrifying. He was wholehearted in his opposition to it. He witnessed the practice of slavery in England and then saw the horrid conditions of this same institution in the American colonies of Georgia and South Carolina. He was told of the beatings African men and women endured that were so severe that they led to death or required months of recovery. Wesley took time to study the trade of enslaved persons that we now call the "Middle Passage" from Africa to Europe to the sugar plantations of the West Indies or the American colonies. He learned the history of this trade and the areas of Africa from which it drew its victims. He then took this information, along with accounts of how enslaved persons were treated in America and put them in his famous tract, "Thoughts Upon Slavery." The second half of that work questions how such actions can be reconciled with the virtues of justice and mercy. Wesley pointed out that the motive behind chattel slavery was simply "to get money." He exhorted the captains of slave ships, merchants, and every person who owned an estate to repent of their involvement in this trade so that they would not lose their souls.[3]

"Thoughts Upon Slavery" was printed and reprinted many times in 1774 and the years that followed both in England and in the American colonies. It was a vehement attack on the practice of chattel slavery. Periodicals that were typically critical of John Wesley and other "enthusiasts" praised the work as one that contained clear facts and relevant observations.

Wesley and the Methodists he led joined other groups in England who were fighting to make the practice of enslavement illegal in the country. They were in the minority, but as their concerns were shared and the facts were detailed, more and more people began to call for an end to this practice. These groups would have to maintain their fortitude until 1807, when the English slave trade was abolished, and continue to hold fast until 1833, when enslaved people in the British Empire were emancipated. When Francis Asbury arrived in America to lead the Methodist movement there, the protest against slavery was shared by its leadership. When they held their Conference in Baltimore in April 1780, they voted "to require those preachers who hold slaves to give promise to set them free." One manuscript continued, "on pain of future exclusion."[4] The Conference went on to "acknowledge that slave-keeping is contrary to the laws of God, man, and nature; and hurtful to society, contrary to the dictates of conscience and pure religion, and doing that which we would not another should do to us."[5]

Methodists had a failure of nerve after the formation of the United States of America. Slavery continued to be seen as a moral evil in the view of northern Methodists. In 1800, a clause was added to the general rules of the church that any preacher who became an owner of an enslaved person would forfeit his credentials. But by 1804 tensions between Methodists in the north and in the south reached a tipping point. A separate *Discipline*, the book that governed the church, was created for the Methodists south of Virginia. The "Section on Slavery," present from the time of Wesley, was removed from this version of the church's book. It was seen as impractical given that the church wanted to continue to grow and expand in the south and receive the giving of southerners, who enjoyed great wealth due to the labor of enslaved persons and the economy they fueled.[6]

When fortitude fails, morals and values are compromised with tragic results. A church that could have influenced those who legally owned enslaved people to emancipate them instead encouraged the practice. A church that could have worked with others to end the institution of slavery in America as it had in England chose silence and conformity. Further, it benefited from the work of enslaved persons whose labor built its church buildings and made many southern Methodists rich.

We are wise to consider where we compromise our values around care of the environment, modern forms of slavery, injustice to those in prison, and a host of other issues in our society and world. It is easy to see the mistakes of those in the past with great clarity and then convince ourselves that we live in a moral gray area that is confounding. Courage enables us to have the strength of self-examination and make sacrifices that arise when we commit ourselves to boldly follow Christ even when sacrifices must be made. This is why Jesus was so clear with his followers when he said,

> "If any want to become my followers, let them deny themselves and take up their cross daily and follow me. For those who want to save their life will lose it, and those who lose their life for my sake will save it. What does it profit them if they gain the whole world, but lose or forfeit themselves?"
>
> (Luke 9:23-25)

Jesus wants us to understand that everyone who follows him will have to pick up a cross of some sort. We should not be surprised that Christ calls us to do hard things. He promised in this text that was a part of following him. When we fail to love our neighbor because of a long-standing tradition of injustice, we fail to pick up the cross Christ has laid before us. Sometimes the cross is the difficulty of loving someone close to you that for some reason is very hard to love. It can be a cross of necessary change in your own life or work around an important issue or group of people that God has called you to undertake. Often, we want to imagine that history held moments when others were asked to undertake an essential issue like suffrage, civil rights, or working to vote a corrupt official out of office, but we assume that Jesus would never bring such an inconvenience as to put such a cross before us. Unwilling to consider the required self-denial of such a task, we assume there is nothing that we personally have to do that requires fortitude. Many live with an ostrich-like ability to not notice all the ways Christ would have them engage important matters in their home, community, or world. By stating that any who want to be his followers must deny themselves, take up their cross daily, and follow him, Jesus communicates that fortitude is an essential virtue in the Christian life.

How much better to use courage for things that matter rather than things that simply do not. Often people seem to be looking for excuses to be bold. "The Great Bull Run" is held in cities in the United States, fashioned after the running of the bulls in Pamplona, Spain, where four thousand to five thousand people run for their lives as a herd of bulls is released and chases them. The website points out, "This event isn't for the faint of heart; participants in the Great Bull Run must enter the race knowing they may be jostled, trampled, bumped, or even gored during the event."[7]

This event is a good example of inconsequential boldness. It does take a certain level of courage to run with the bulls. But even if you successfully run with the bulls, it does not matter. Once the adrenaline rush wears off, it makes no difference.

Meanwhile, there are places in your life and in the world where God is calling you and me to have the fortitude to accept a calling of God that is both challenging and meaningful. Jesus uses an image well-known in the Roman world, the cross. It was an instrument of death. He calls his followers not only to self-denial but also to die to themselves as they take up their cross daily.

Fortitude is necessary for Christians, because Jesus calls us to a life where we sacrifice for others. Imagine how different families would be if people were willing to love each other in bold ways. Imagine how much faster conflicts would resolve if people would have the boldness to address them. Consider how many problems in our community could be overcome if citizens would boldly unite to deal with them. I wonder how many visions God has given to individuals and churches about sharing the gospel, blessing the poor, or working for justice that would become reality if Christians drew their strength from God and demonstrated the strength of fortitude. When we lack fortitude, we consider the challenges I just listed to be as nonsensical as the entry form for the Bull Run.

FORTITUDE IS NECESSARY FOR CHRISTIANS, BECAUSE JESUS CALLS US TO A LIFE WHERE WE SACRIFICE FOR OTHERS.

Most of us are not signing up for the challenges I just listed any more than we are going to sign up for the Bull Run. That is often due to an underestimation of our strength and the capacity of God to work in and through our lives. Yet when we hear a calling for something that really matters, it can lead people to make the greatest of sacrifices for others. Fortitude longs to be called forth because humans long to know that their lives counted for something.

When Winston Churchill became the British prime minister in 1940, morale was at an all-time low. After just a few weeks of battle, Hitler's armies had conquered Holland, Luxembourg, and Belgium. Paris fell on June 14. Three days later, the French requested an armistice, a polite way of saying they surrendered.

The following day, June 18, Churchill spoke to the House of Commons about the disastrous turn of events in Europe. Churchill exercised candor with England's leaders and citizens. Britain now stood alone against the seemingly unstoppable German army, commanded by Adolph Hitler, a fascist intent on global domination.

Churchill updated the British people on the status of the war. The news was bad, but the British army, navy, and air force were still strong after the heroic evacuation of British forces at Dunkirk. When Churchill ended his speech, he helped his people understand that everything was at stake, and they must rise to the occasion. He stated,

> I expect that the Battle of Britain is about to begin. Upon this battle depends the survival of Christian civilization. Upon it depends our own British life, and the long continuity of our institutions and our Empire. The whole fury and might of the enemy must very soon be turned on us. Hitler knows that he will have to break us in this Island or lose the war. If we can stand up to him, all Europe may be free and the life of the world may move forward into broad, sunlit uplands. But if we fail, then the whole world, including the United States, including all that we have known and cared for, will sink into the abyss of a new Dark Age made more sinister, and perhaps more protracted, by the lights of perverted science. Let us therefore brace ourselves to our duties, and so bear ourselves that, if the British Empire and its Commonwealth last for a thousand years, men will still say, "This was their finest hour."[8]

Churchill told his nation of its coming epic struggle. He called out their courage. He trusted their fortitude was sufficient to secure their role in history as those who saved democracy and the free world.

Those words transformed the people of Britain. They were no longer a beleaguered nation. They were an emboldened people who went on to win the war.

We can pick up our cross and endure its hardship when we recognize it is simply necessary for the good of those that we love to do so. In the causes that God calls us to undertake, we will be given strength if we exercise fortitude and understand the importance of what God asks of us when we take our life seriously. Some people have to live this way every single day due to the color of their skin or the economic condition of their country. While some Christians pick up a cross only on occasion and may struggle to identify any real hardship in their life, others move from cross to cross to cross as they deal with hardships that require sacrifice for themselves and those they love daily.

A CASE STUDY IN FORTITUDE

In Sierra Leone, Africa, there are a thousand reasons to give up. My friend John Yambasu—bishop, father, church builder, world changer—loved his country and never gave up working for a better life for the people of Sierra Leone.

We met in 1997. I was there on a church trip and Rev. John Yambasu was our host. The first thing I noticed was that John got his hands dirty. Mixing cement in a country near the equator is taxing work. We each had shovels and worked together turning over the concrete mix, gravel, and water. In that heat we had only a short time before the material hardened. A few hours of this and we were covered in sweat and grime, equally committed to being the last man standing, and fast friends.

We were working on a building that had been damaged months earlier by rebel soldiers. The bullet marks were visible on the walls that were still standing. As we worked together, John told me about the endemic poverty, sky-high unemployment rate, piecemeal health care few could afford to access, and history of government corruption that were all contributing factors to the war. I began to feel overwhelmed. The hot sun, the weight of the cement as the hours passed, and the magnitude of the issues in Sierra Leone weighed heavily on me. By contrast, John continued to mix the cement with ease, and he remained joyful in spirit.

COURAGE THAT ENDURES IN HARDSHIP IS CALLED FORTITUDE.

Courage that endures in hardship is called fortitude. And fortitude, there in the sun with our hands covered in cement, fortitude was called John.

He possessed a deep faith and an ebullient way about him. He would sometimes answer questions with hymns. At one point, I asked, "How will you finish this building?"

John said, "Well, we will have to trust that God will provide the resources. It may take some time, but I know the Lord is watching over us right now and sees the need."

I thought, "Great, no plan. This is never going anywhere."

I said, "That must be difficult."

I think he read my mind and could feel my judgment. He smiled and said, "Pastor," emphasizing this word to remind me that faith was to be expected from a pastor, "do you know that hymn that says, 'When we walk with the Lord in the light of his word, what a glory he sheds on our way…'?"

Before I knew it, we were singing "Trust and Obey" while laying a new course of cinder blocks. It had never occurred to me that people lived this way, singing hymns to remind themselves to trust God where they could not see how the future would unfold. I lived in a different world. John was walking with the Lord, trusting that God would provide.

John's faith was a courageous faith, because he had no reserve, no backup plan, and no safety net for his life. He trusted God because God was what he had.

Members of my congregation heard about John's efforts to heal his war-torn home, and they were asking how they could help. God used that time to place a deep conviction in my friend's life. He was morally offended by the severity of the war. When villages were burned, parents were often executed in front of their children. Sometimes the rebels forced children to kill their own families before making them child soldiers. John felt God's call to help these children. We worked with him to start the Child Rescue Centre (CRC), whose initial mission was to care for children living on the streets after the war. Back in Sierra Leone, John put on his clerical collar and went out at night with two staff members to gather children sleeping under market tables.

I would see this same force at work over the years. The calling of God often showed my friend what was possible when all anyone could tell him is that his ideas were impossible. His fortitude, based on a deep trust in God's ability to do anything God desired, called him into action. I recall him asking me one time how people in the United States could not find it morally offensive that any child would have to beg for food, sleep without shelter, lack proper care from adults, or not know the love of Christ. He had a way of speaking with candor that convicted but left you looking forward to the next conversation.

Through the years of working in partnership with John—who has now become Bishop Yambasu—I was able to see him often in meetings held to develop the work of the CRC and Mercy Hospital, the small hospital that serves thousands of people annually. His courage gave him the confidence to dream of the future and invite us to dream with him. Rather than see limitations, we saw what was possible. Those possibilities became the projects we agreed to pursue together, such as developing Mercy Hospital in ways that would better serve its focus on child and maternal health.

Jesus washed his disciples' feet and told his followers to do likewise. Bishop Yambasu heard that call and lived it out as servanthood. His fortitude was demonstrated in his willingness to do the hard things. He led his church to take on new challenges, like creating a seminary or rebuilding a hospital that had been abandoned years earlier.

Another example of his willingness to face a difficult reality and have the endurance to find a solution emerged around the conflict in The UMC over LGBTQ inclusion. Rather than assume that the conflict could not be resolved, Bishop Yambasu made an unusual move. Working on his own, he brought together a global group of leaders in The United Methodist Church to create the "Protocol of Reconciliation and Grace Through Separation" in 2019. Observing Bishop Yambasu during those meetings, I was again able to appreciate the way my friend's fortitude enabled him to endure the difficulties of this conversation. He continued to encourage us to have hope that we could find an acceptable resolution, even when that seemed impossible. His faith and leadership called us to do our best work in keeping with our shared love of Christ. There were times when his prayer enabled us to take the next faithful step in negotiations and envision a future full of ministry and free of the conflict that has so hampered the work of the denomination in recent years.

It was an early Sunday morning when I received the news that Bishop Yambasu had been killed in an automobile accident in Sierra Leone. I was so stunned I did not know what to say. After the call, I began to think about our last meal together months earlier. We had laughed as we recounted so many things the Lord had called us to do together. We had taken risks, had candid conversations. We had endured through hardships. We had held on to hope when things went wrong. We celebrated each other, our friendship, and the goodness of the church that brought us together. Looking back on that time now, I realize the only thing I neglected to do was to tell John that he was one of the most courageous men I had ever known. Perhaps that is the gift of considering courage on these pages. It puts the gift of his life in perspective.

They buried Bishop John Yambasu on the site of the seminary at Leicester Peak in the exact spot where our friendship began twenty-three years earlier. In his life Bishop John Yambasu endured great hardship, sacrifice, and loss. Yet his faith never wavered. God gave him a vision that enabled him to start and develop project after project, and touch life after life. All of this was possible because he exhibited the long-enduring power of Christian fortitude.

Chapter 6

THE LOVE
OF COURAGE

Jesus said, "There was a man who had two sons.
The younger of them said to his father, 'Father,
give me the share of the property that will belong
to me.' So he divided his property between them.
A few days later the younger son gathered all he
had and traveled to a distant country, and there he
squandered his property in dissolute living."

(Luke 15:11-13)

A few years ago I was walking with my family on the National
Seashore area of the Outer Banks of North Carolina. We were looking
at shells, picking them up, and deciding which ones to keep and which
ones to leave. Focused intently on the sand before me, I was startled

when I realized that we had come across a sailboat, unceremoniously resting on its side in the dry sand. No one was around. I thought, "Somebody had a bad day." Later I learned that somebody had a bad night. A man bought two sailboats in New Jersey that had been damaged by Hurricane Sandy. He was sailing one and towing the other to South Carolina for repairs. He was about seven miles offshore the Outer Banks and sailing alone when he fell asleep. The wind shifted. It gently blew him in to shore. He woke up about the time the keel of the boat hit the sand. It was high tide. The sailboat was carried up onto the beach. As the water receded, it was impossible to move it back out to sea.

We walked up to the boat to get a closer look. There were articles strewn about, as though there had been a break-in to the cabin. It appeared that some fixtures had been stripped from the boat. A homemade sign read,

> NOT SALVAGE
> This is my home.
> I am trying to get off this beach!

I think about that sailboat and its owner sometimes. At one time or another, I think most people try to figure out how to get off the beach where they have floundered and abruptly come to a rest. In such moments it is important to remember that we are not salvage. We should not be sold for parts, left as wreckage, or labeled derelict.

We must find the courage to figure out how to get back to the deep water, where we can continue on our journey.

Jesus told a story about a man who had two sons. In this parable, he helps us consider the way that courage and love catalyze each other and enable us to find our way.

THE YOUNGER SON

The younger son did not realize it, but his sailboat had run aground. It is interesting how long it can take us to figure out that something has gone desperately wrong in life before we react. In the case of the younger son, he began to wake up when a great famine came to the land. His money was spent, jobs were scarce, and he became hungry. He found a job working for a guy who raised pigs. When Jesus told this story and used the word *pigs*, I think you would have heard either a gasp or a moan in the Jewish crowd. In any culture pigs are dirty animals. In Judaism, they are ritually unclean. They are forbidden. You don't eat pork. You don't touch swine. If your job is caring for pigs, you are belly-up on the beach. With this one detail, Jesus's audience knows that the younger son is far, far from home.

One day the younger son felt hunger so great that when he looked at the pigs' slop he thought, *You know, that does not look half bad. Maybe with some hot sauce . . .* This was a personal wake-up call. In that moment, the younger son does something that is so courageous that some go a lifetime without ever doing it. He became candid with himself about the situation his decisions created. He realizes two truths. First, he has missed the mark of adult life. He launched, only to go askew and blow up seconds from the launchpad. His failure is so severe that he believes it has destroyed the relationship he once enjoyed with his father. He believes he has lost his identity as his father's son. He decides he will say: "Father, I have sinned against heaven and before you; I am no longer worthy to be called your son; treat me like one of your hired hands" (Luke 15:18-19).

"I am no longer worthy to be called your son" is a powerful statement about an opportunity of a lifetime squandered. The younger son believes that he has blown his relationship with his father apart.

He realizes a second truth: it is better to be a servant in his father's house than spend one more day in the pigsty of his own making. It takes courage to undertake the long walk home and to ask his father to take him back, even as a servant. The only reason the younger son is able to consider this is that he knows that love is a key virtue of his father's character. The expectation of kindness from his father animates his courage.

The younger son began the journey back home. I doubt that his low expectations slowed his pace. Becoming a servant in the home where he grew up was a drastically diminished status, but it was better than anything he had found for himself. Heading home means the younger son has the fortitude not to give up. He has not allowed an inner voice that might convince him that he has reached the end of the line to dominate his thoughts. Courage enables us to put one foot in front of the other, to take the next faithful step to some form of a new life. That courage is in part based on the hope that his father might still hold enough love to offer him just enough to start again.

I once knew a younger son. His name was Tim. He wandered into a church service with his grandmother one Sunday. He sat in the back. Rather than sit in her usual spot, his grandmother, a pillar in that church, sat next to him in the pew. When a pillar moves her seat, everything feels off balance. I knew something special was happening. Tim and I developed a relationship. I learned that Tim had recently entered into recovery from a drug and alcohol addiction. He used to ask me if things he was doing were normal. "Is it normal to look forward to quitting time at work?" "Is it normal to be upset if your girlfriend takes your money without telling you?"

One day I asked him why he asked me what was normal so often. "Pastor," he said, "I have been getting drunk and doing drugs so long,

I've got no idea how people do life without it. I have to learn all about normal if I'm ever going to be normal."

I learned that Tim was living with his grandmother. I asked her one day why Tim was not living with his mother and she said, "She wouldn't have him after all that he had done before. Neither would anyone else. He didn't have any place to go and he was living in his car. But I heard he was getting help with his problems. I got a message to him. I told him to come over to see me. After we talked, he stayed."

Over the time I knew Tim, he was exceedingly attentive to his grandmother. Even after he was doing so well in his job that he was able to pay his past bills and get a place of his own, he stopped by daily to check on her and do chores around her house. I complimented him on the care he showed her one day. Tim said, "That old woman saved my life. She made a bet on me that I wouldn't have made. She took a risk on me that no one else was willing to take. She kept me in line. She loved me so much it convinced me that I could make a life for myself."

There is a relationship between courage, love, and restoration. If the younger son never comes to his senses, it is very hard to help him. It takes courage for him to do that. It also takes courage for others to take a risk on him. When people we love act in ways that violate our values, squander our resources, or disappoint our sense of right and wrong, we need courage if we are to continue to love them. The fear that has to be overcome is whether they will disappoint us again.

THE LOVING FATHER

"He set off and went to his father. But while he was still far off, his father saw him and was filled with compassion; he ran and put his arms around him and kissed him. Then the son said to him, 'Father, I have sinned against heaven and before you; I am no longer worthy to be called your son.'"

(Luke 5:20-21)

Many have said that the parable of the prodigal son is actually the parable of the loving father. The parable is among the greatest stories ever told, not only because of the characters involved, but also because of the human dynamics it observes. Jesus shows us what it means to be embraced and loved, especially when we think we are no longer worthy of love from others. The loving father pays little attention to the self-evaluation offered by his son. He calls for a fresh robe to be put on the son who returns home in filthy tatters and a ring for the finger of the son he feared was dead. This ring is not costume jewelry. It is a symbol of family identity. The younger son may have pawned his original family seal when his fortune was used up. Replacing this ring is a great act of love, because it reestablishes an identity the younger son thought was gone forever.

THERE IS NO FORM OF LOVE THAT DOES NOT REQUIRE SOME LEVEL OF COURAGE.

It is a parent's love that propels courage in the life of the father to take this risk on his son. Courage and love are virtues that are integral to each other. There is no form of love that does not require some level of courage. To love is to be vulnerable. To be vulnerable is to take risks. I recall asking a girl to a dance in the eighth grade. It should not have been that hard. She was a neighbor and a friend. But I had never asked a girl to a dance. She was also several rungs beyond me on the middle school social ladder. The closer I got to the point of speaking with her, the more fear expressed itself. As I approached her locker, my pulse increased. My mouth dried out. I could feel my heart pounding. I was fairly certain that by the time I asked, "Uhhhh, I was, uhhhh, wondering if, uhhhhh, you would maybe, I mean if you wanted to, uhhhh, go with me to the dance?" she might have to hold a paper bag over my mouth to control my imminent hyperventilation. As it turned out, I found the courage to ask and she was kind enough to accept my invitation, but it was a wild ride for my autonomic nervous system.

The courage implicit to vulnerability extends far beyond adolescent affection. Every human relationship is the testing of connection, closeness, and intimacy. In relationships there is a movable relational line that each person pushes further and further along as he or she tests many factors, such as compatibility, capacity to handle disagreement, the pleasure of one's company, common interests, dependability, empathy, and more. Each push of this line takes us further along a winding journey of knowledge of the other, of trust and intimacy.

When the younger son misspent his inheritance, he betrayed his father's trust. Using the inheritance in a way that communicated a lack of appreciation for his father's work and life was a violation of trust that is not easy to reestablish. It was the equivalent of a rejection of not only his father's love, but his father's life. This began the moment the son asked for his inheritance before his father was dead. Squandering this wealth only added insult to injury. To allow the younger son back into the family was an act of risk and vulnerability.

Rejection by another person is difficult for us, not only because it creates a boundary on the closeness we experience with that person, but because it feels like a judgment of our life and its value. If a family member or friend rejects us in some way, we never know if it is temporary or permanent. Whether it is a cooling or a rebuff of the relationship, we are prone to feel as though we came up short. This vulnerability is found in all human relationships. We can experience it in marriages, dating, friendships, relationships between parents and children, connections between colleagues, and bonds between siblings. To open oneself to be known, and seek to know another, requires courage that must exhibit itself over and over as relational bids are made, the boundary of intimacy is moved, and risks are taken over the years and decades the relationship is shared.

The loving father is important to us because he demonstrates the motivation love brings to courage. It is remarkable how often people are willing to take a risk on someone they love to see if a relationship can be reestablished or renewed.

Ian Pitt-Watson, a professor at Fuller Seminary, once said, "Some things are loved because they are worthy; some things are worthy because they are loved."[1]

Many people have some possession that they love because of its value. A piece of jewelry from a grandmother, a newer car, a baseball coach who has a gifted pitcher all make the list of things loved because they are worthy.

But some things are worthy because they are loved. We used to have a dog like that. Woody was about ten years old when we found him at a dog rescue event. His habits were already formed. This included his fear of men and his near refusal to enter our house when the door was held wide open for him. Experiencing Woody's many fears helped us understand why he had never found his "forever home." Woody knew no commands. He did not do tricks. He was clearly not the sharpest tack in the box. But there was something more going on. Our theory was that he had been abused. His anxiety was so notable that we guessed the abuser was probably a man. Whoever did this clearly did not want him to enter the house. Paul says that love is patient and kind.

I know it took several weeks and two large bags of dog food before Woody was comfortable with any contact from me.

Our daughter Kathryn loved that dog. She played with him daily. They ran around the yard. She hugged him. The more love she conferred on that dog, the smarter he became. One day Kathryn called me outside. "Watch this," she said. She threw a ball. Woody bounded after it, picked it up, and joyfully returned it. I said, "Kathryn, it's a miracle. You have performed brain surgery on a dog!"

Woody remained shy, but he grew to be happy and at peace. He liked to play ball with us. He got excited when we came home. He never fully trusted men, but he took me in. He learned he was a part of our family and that made it easier to cross the threshold. Over time, Woody became more the dog God intended him to be.

"Some things are loved because they are worthy; some things are worthy because they are loved."

The loving father in Jesus's parable demonstrates that we are both. We are loved because we are worthy as children of God. We are worthy because we are loved. Even though we are sinful and separated from God, Christ has, through his death and resurrection, offered us assurance that we can experience forgiveness, love, and new life. This love is a dependable factor when we are fearful or experience despair.

There is a beaded cross on my desk that reminds me of this fact. It was made by Don when he was a child. When Don was a teenager, he was diagnosed with cancer. It is not easy to see a teenager go through chemotherapy and radiation. He should have been in the most vital years of his life, but instead lost energy and strength. Don suffered. His parents suffered. We all prayed for a miracle of healing that never came. He persisted courageously, but eventually died. After his funeral his mother gave me the beaded cross that her son had made years earlier.

She asked me to remember her son. I laid the cross Don made on my desk the next day. That was many years ago, and I have never been able to move it. Few things are more challenging to belief in God's power and love than the death of a young person. I have often wondered why I have left that cross in place. I believe that it has become a means not only to remember Don, but to remember that the love of Christ never faltered for him. That cross gives me assurance that Don now experiences an eternal form of God's love present in the Resurrection. It reminds me to have the courage of the young man I witnessed as he cared and encouraged his parents and friends in light of his illness and impending death. That cross reminds me that the love of Christ bears all things, hopes all things, and endures all things. When I am fearful or anxious, that cross centers me. Its reminder that I am loved gives me courage.

Jesus shares this parable in part to remind us of the power of love, the power of acceptance, and the way it gives us the confidence to continue in life, no matter how far away we have wandered from home. This is a great blessing for the courage and fortitude we need, especially when we are in the dark and despairing portions of life.

WHEREVER YOU GO

The thought that courage in the Christian life is initiated by the knowledge that we are loved might seem to be at odds with what we find in the Bible. For instance, when Moses died and Joshua took over as the leader of Israel, it appears that he felt a bit overwhelmed. This may be why the Lord told Joshua three times, "Be strong and courageous." The Lord says,

"I hereby command you: Be strong and courageous;
do not be frightened or dismayed, for the Lᴏʀᴅ your
God is with you wherever you go."

(Joshua 1:9)

But notice that the power of the Lord's message is not in the command, "Be strong and courageous." Joshua lacks confidence that he is adequate to the task. If that were not the case, the Lord would not need to have this conversation. Joshua's insecurity is something you can't simply command away. The essential aspect of the Lord's message to him is the crucial assurance that, "I [am] with you wherever you go."

That is God's love message to Joshua. It's what he needs to know if he is to have the courage necessary to move into the Promised Land. We see the same message on the other end of the Bible, where Paul shares his testimony. The Lord has gotten this message to him as well. In his Letter to the Romans, Paul writes, "I am convinced that neither death nor life, nor angels, nor rulers, nor things present, nor things to come, nor powers, nor height, nor depth, nor anything else in all creation, will be able to separate us from the love of God in Christ Jesus our Lord" (Romans 8:38-39).

WHEN WE ARE CONVINCED THAT WE ARE DEARLY LOVED BY GOD, WHEN WE ARE BOLD IN GOD'S LOVE, WE ARE LIKELY TO BE COURAGEOUS IN LIFE.

When you and I believe these words, the likelihood that we will demonstrate courage grows exponentially. When we are convinced that we are dearly loved by God, when we are bold in God's love, we are likely to be courageous in life. When we are convinced of God's love for us, we will more readily demonstrate the fortitude that endures the hardship of the bad places in life.

A SENSE OF LOVE AND TRUST

Jesus's good news of God's love for us is so radical that many find it hard to believe. Jesus's parable paints a picture of the surprising nature of love. We see the younger son on the road, watching his father run toward him. He hasn't seen his father move this fast in years. I have to believe that the younger son was not necessarily surprised by his father's words but may have been stunned by his father's embrace. This tangible expression of love, an act of celebration that the son thought gone and dead was present and alive, was a spontaneous celebration of his life.

There are many reasons some find it hard to believe that they are loved. Some people do not learn that they are loved in their family of origin. Love may not have been extended in any formative way. Worse yet, a person may be a victim of trauma, abuse, or neglect growing up in an unsafe family system. When this occurs, victims sometimes lose their sense of self. They are oriented to fear and anxiety rather than confidence and self-worth. Such an experience can be a significant obstacle to personal development, including the virtues of courage and love that are more likely to flourish in environments of safety, security, and care.

Others find that their race, culture, or status as an immigrant leaves them with systemic societal messages that they are not trusted or welcomed.

I have a friend who is a pastor who opened my eyes to the ways people of different races experience our community. "As a white person, you never have to think about your race. As an African American man, I have to think about it every day."

"Can you give me an example of that?" I asked.

"When I take a walk in my neighborhood, I never leave my home without a driver's license. Do you ever do that?" he asked.

"I can't recall ever thinking I needed to do that," I said. "Why do you take your license?"

He laughed as he said, "That is a question only a white person would ask. I take it because on two occasions, while walking on a sidewalk in my neighborhood after I got home from the church in the evening, a police cruiser has come alongside me. The officer has one question: 'May I ask what you are doing in this neighborhood?' That's when I pull out my driver's license to show him that I live in this neighborhood and that I am taking a walk for my exercise. Now let me ask, has that ever happened to you in your entire life?"

The answer would be "no."

Think of the fortitude it takes for those who receive cumulative messages that they are unworthy of love, care, or trust to go through life, believing that the world holds opportunity they can enjoy. Consider how difficult it is to develop the capacity to be confident and successful when so many have given them messages that they are less than everyone else. When a person with this life experience enters a church and hears a pastor say that they are loved by God, it can sound unbelievable. It may remind them of the email that tells you that someone on another continent wants to send you millions of dollars because you are known to be a very smart and trusted individual. If only you will send all your bank information, they will make this grand deposit. Too good to be true usually is. The message of God's love for us is not spam.

A MOTHER'S LOVE

The loving father knows that he must instill confidence in his son if he is going to have the capacity to truly start over in life. He calls for a banquet to be prepared. This will be a day of celebration. By holding a meal, inviting family, friends, and employees, the loving father is helping everyone understand that the status his son once enjoyed is his again. The father's love has no interest in shame or guilt. He wants his son to regain his sense of community and realize that his standing as a son is not lost.

When we believe that God loves us, we enter a place of courage. The knowledge of such love creates a foundation of confidence on which courage stands. It enables us to know that we can be vulnerable with others because their acceptance or rejection will neither increase nor diminish the love we offer others.

One afternoon I was sitting in an airport. A mother was walking with her son, who appeared to be about two years old. He was one of those little boys who looks like he possesses an old soul. He was having a big time. He waved to everyone he passed. He slowly made his way down the concourse, smiling and waving, like he was in a parade. At one point a little girl walked past with her dad in the other direction. I bet she was about three. She was the little boy's height. His eyes grew large, like he had never before seen anyone his size. He was amazed and so happy. He stopped, put his hands on his knees, leaned over, and gave her a giant smile. He turned his head in pace with her as she walked past.

I thought about this little boy later and considered what would happen if that same child would walk down the concourse alone, without his mother. What if his mother walked so far ahead of her son that he could not see her? Would you still get the smiles and waves? I don't think so. He would probably default to fear, which would come out in tears, or anger, which might also come out in tears. This is what is great about two-year-olds, they keep it simple and they keep it real. So, the key to the way he treated everyone to a smile and wave is not his winning personality, but his mother's love. He knows his mother is with him. He knows he is secure in her love. She will not leave him or abandon him. In his security of her love, he has the courage to risk connecting to all of us.

God uses people around us to make us secure in love. This is the gift of community found in family, friendships, neighborhoods, churches, and other networks of relationships God uses to remind us that we are loved. As a result, we can love others.

> **GOD USES PEOPLE AROUND US TO MAKE US SECURE IN LOVE. . . . AS A RESULT, WE CAN LOVE OTHERS.**

HOW TO LOVE

If we want people to grow in courage, we are wise to find ways to convince them that they are loved. Like the loving father, when we love others intentionally, we are placing courage in their lives. We encourage as we speak of how their strengths and gifts can be used to advance an important cause, solve an important problem, care for someone, or speak out when it is safer to be silent. We must love in such a way that courage grows in others. If you wonder how to build confidence in others through love, consider these ideas.

Speak Words that Honor

My wife and I have attended a lot of wedding rehearsal dinners over the years.

The best wedding rehearsal dinners are focused on honor. During one such occasion, the groom's mother came to the microphone with a small booklet. She said, "Kenneth made this for me when he was in the third grade. It is a booklet called, 'The Reason I Love You.' Each page starts with the phrase, 'I love you because...' Let me read you just a few."

After she read the endearing words of her third-grade son describing why he loved his mother, she picked up a second book. "Kenneth, your father and I decided to write you a book too. It is also called, 'We Love You Because...'" Then she read, "We love you because you are a friend. The little boys you played with as a child are your groomsmen today. You have supported and cared for each other your whole life. We love you because you love our family. When you were in your twenties and agreed to coach your little brother's basketball team, missing social events to do so, you were his hero and ours too. We love you because of the way that you care for Lila..."

Hearing the careful way this couple honored their son was a tender moment. It had a powerful effect. The next day groomsmen and bridesmaids alike told me that they dropped embarrassing tales that they planned to share and instead offered words of appreciation for the friendship and love the bride or groom had offered them over the years. These stories and remarks cast the bride and groom in the warm glow of honor. The families honored each other for the children they raised and the way each loved the other's child. There was humor. There was mirth, but never at anyone's expense. The bride and groom knew, by the end of the evening, that they were highly esteemed by those dearest to them. In return, they shared their love for their families and those in the wedding party.

Such words of love have the capacity to instill confidence that leads to courage. You don't have to have a dinner to share words of honor. You can write the words on a note or say them over a cup of coffee. The key is to consider your remarks and make time to deliver them. Courage is often needed when the pursuit of a calling is highly stressful or when we reach a personal low point of defeat that includes despair or depression. In such moments it can be hard to remember that God loves us. But we can remember the words of the people right around us. Words of honor are best offered before difficulty begins. They are a protective armor we wear in life. They are also magnetic. They draw us back to the people we need to remind us of who we really are in difficult times.

The Spartans thought courage was best formed by dropping their children in the wilderness and telling them to figure it out. I think courage can also be formed when we gather around a person and start true sentences with "I love you because…"

Make It Special

I was giving out a student leadership award to a graduate for a civic organization in the small community where we lived. I was asked to come to the graduation early to do a sound check and review the program with other speakers. It was a remarkably pleasant June evening. We were sitting in folding chairs on the football field. There was a newly constructed grandstand where diplomas would be given.

It was festooned in the school colors. The scaffolding underneath was hidden by fabric. I looked up the hill where a long procession of graduates were making their way down the steps to take their chairs. There was blue and gold bunting that ran across the chain link fence. It provided a striking backdrop for the graduates. I noticed that the chairs were placed so that they made straight and exact rows. I turned to the principal, who was sitting next to me, and said, "You all have done a great job with this graduation. Everything looks so nice." I went on to observe what I noticed to her.

She smiled and said, "It's nice of you to notice. We tried to do a little extra for this graduation. We think it is really important."

I was curious about the word *really* and said, "Graduations are important, but it sounds like you mean more than that."

She said, "I do. About 40 percent of these kids will go on to get a college degree. They will do this again. But most will not. For most of them, this will be the only event where their family gathers around them to tell them they are proud of them. This will mark one of the only formal occasions in their lives where a congratulatory word will be spoken to them. Many will get married. That is another opportunity. Then they will get jobs, and after working forty to fifty years, there will be nothing more than a final pay stub. Not even a letter of appreciation. There certainly will be no gold watch. But look at them tonight." She pointed at the procession moving closer to where we were sitting. "They are smiling. Now look behind you. Their parents are grateful and happy as they watch and wave. Tonight, the focus is on the graduates. That is why we think it is really important for this to be nice."

It is a very odd world when people can conceivably count the events in life where they were the focal point on one hand. It was not long after that experience that I developed the "Berlin Salute" for our daughters. If one of them did something special, like scored a goal in soccer or a made good grade in a difficult class, or if we caught them being kind or compassionate to someone, they would get the Berlin Salute at dinner. "Sarah," I would say in a booming voice, "it has been brought to the attention of the family that today you did well on a science test that you were certain you were going to fail. Not only did you not fail, you managed to get a B+ after doing a considerable amount of hard work over the last three days and during the rest of the semester. For this the family would like to confer upon you the Berlin Salute." At this point the rest of the family knew to stand, face the honoree, and say, "Saaaalute!" in unison while saluting her with their right hand.

ACTS OF LOVE LEAVE A MARK.

Find your own tradition. Catch people being good. Congratulate them when they have a win. There will come a day when they will need to remember that there was a time when they got the salute. There was a time when someone wrote them a note or told them detailed reasons that they were really special. Those reasons create a sense of identity and confidence that builds courage over time. Such acts of love leave a mark. They make it far more likely that the recipient will take the risk to offer love and encouragement to others.

Remind People You Love and Believe in Them

When persons lose courage, they are often losing belief in themselves as valid actors in whatever arena they are standing. They may still believe in the cause for which they once fought, but they will also begin to think that they should give up so that they won't get in the way of the good they hope to do. One by one strengths and spiritual gifts are dropped to the ground. Our warriors just want to hit the showers and go home. In such moments it is essential to quickly and directly tell these persons that you believe in them and you expect them to believe in themselves as well.

A friend's grandson was struggling with online education during the global pandemic. Second grade was just not going well for him. She was talking with her daughter when Joe burst into the kitchen in tears.

Christina, his mother, did not miss a beat. She looked at her son and said: "What do I tell you?"

Joe: "That I can do hard things."

Christina: "And why can you do that?"

Joe: (sniffling) "Because you love me."

Christina: "And do you believe that I love you?

Joe: (sniffling again) "Yes."

Christina: "I do love you. You are very smart, and you are a hard worker. You can do this. Now get back down to your desk."

Joe: "OK. Can we have lunch soon?"

Christina: "Absolutely."

Use this level of simplicity and clarity. And it never hurts to throw lunch in as well!

Pray for Them

Betty is a retired woman I know. She is gentle and kind. She is hardworking and wise. She sent me a text after hearing a message I shared about loving people who were hard to love.

Betty: "Your message today, for me, was so very true. When my son was in the throes of addiction, I was becoming afraid I was losing love for him. I began a prayer regimen that I could: accept him, treat him with respect, dignity, compassion, and love. This I did for months, maybe years. Today he and I have a beautiful relationship truly based on love. One of the miracles in my life through God."

My text: "Wow that is a powerful testimony. God is good all the time. Can I share that to encourage others?"

Her text: "Absolutely. Just celebrated my twenty-fifth anniversary in Al-Anon."

That last bit of information is important. Betty found Al-Anon when her courage was beginning to fail. In that community she learned what she could do for her son and what she could not. She had to gain the courage to both love her son and draw boundaries that would keep her son's addiction from destroying her life. The Al-Anon community was a place where she felt loved and accepted. They gave her the confidence to learn to pray in a new way. That prayer did something powerful in her life. It restored a mother's love. It put up functional boundaries. It gave her the ability to turn outward and love her son in a new way.

THE POWER OF LOVE

The younger son returned home with little courage or confidence, other than what he assumed about the loving nature of his father's character that might allow him to live as a servant on his property. That love was like a homing beacon that brought him to a safe harbor. It inspired the courage he needed to take those first awkward steps that lead us to a new life.

People all around you are trying to do hard things. They are following their calling. They are managing the complexity of life in many ways. Some seem to do it effortlessly. But most find that fortitude can falter when the pressure is high or the road to achieve our goal is longer than we ever imagined it would be. We have the opportunity to give people the good news of God's love for them. We have the capacity to show them how their life makes a difference now and name how God may use it to do some significant task or change some important issue in the future. It is essential that we know we are loved. Imagine what might happen if we shared that love in such a way that the people around us would gain courage.

Jesus's ministry enabled people to experience the love of God in tangible ways. His teaching comforts us in its assurance that if we are lost, God will search until we are found. It also challenges us to center our lives on his rule of love so that we will do courageous things to extend the kingdom of God. With courage, we clarify what our life is about and gain conviction about the people we are called to bless and the issues we are called to address in life. We cling to our hope in Christ, understanding that only with the ongoing power of the Holy Spirit and an active relationship with the resurrected Christ, we will have the capacity to sustain our courage. The complexities of the world and the difficulties encountered when we undertake a noble effort require us to not only have faith in God but also remain deeply committed to the calling God provided that necessitated courage in the first place. The love Jesus commanded when he said, "Just as I have loved you, you also should love one another" (John 13:34) is the string that ties this bundle of elements found in courage together. Knowing that we are loved and knowing that we are expected by our Lord to live in loving ways is both the foundation and the proper outcome of courage. Jesus calls us to be courageous people, so that we will live life fully and use our lives to bless the people around us and the world in which we live.

NOTES

Chapter 1: The Clarity of Courage

1. "About John Lewis," Humanity in Action USA, https://www
   .humanityinaction.org/fellowship-john-lewis/about-john-lewis/.
   Accessed September 18, 2020.
2. John Lewis, *Across That Bridge: Life Lessons and a Vision for Change*
   (New York: Hachette Books, 2017), 91.
3. John Lewis, *Across That Bridge*, 80.
4. "About John Lewis," Humanity in Action USA. Accessed September 18,
   2020.
5. John Lewis, "Together, You Can Redeem the Soul of Our Nation,"
   The New York Times, July 30, 2020, https://www.nytimes.com/2020
   /07/30/opinion/john-lewis-civil-rights-america.html. Accessed
   November 2, 2020.

Chapter 2: The Conviction of Courage

1. E. W. Blandy, "Where He Leads Me," *The United Methodist Hymnal*
   (Nashville: The United Methodist Publishing House, 1989), 338,
   refrain.

Chapter 3: The Candor of Courage

1. Cathy Free, "A couple was shamed for their aging house. Hundreds of people stepped in to help spruce it up," *The Washington Post*, August 27, 2020, https://www.washingtonpost.com/lifestyle /2020/08/27/couple-was-shamed-their-aging-house-hundreds -people-stepped-help-spruce-it-up/. Accessed November 3, 2020.

2. Fred B. Craddock, *Luke. Interpretation: A Bible Commentary for Teaching and Preaching*; edited by James Luther Mays (Louisville: John Knox Press, 1990), 104-106.

Chapter 4: The Hope of Courage

1. "Lost Friends ads reveal the heartbreak of family separation during slavery," Molly Reid Cleaver, editor, *The Historic New Orleans Collection Quarterly*, Fall 2018, https://www.hnoc.org /publications/first-draft/lost-friends-ads-reveal-heartbreak-family -separation-during-slavery. Accessed November 4, 2020.

2. "Kennedy Flame Put Out Accidentally by Pupils," *The New York Times*, December 11, 1963, https://www.nytimes.com/1963/12/11/archives /kennedy-flame-put-out-accidentally-by-pupils. Accessed November 4, 2020.

3. Robert Robinson, "Come Thou Fount of Every Blessing," stanza 2, http://hymnbook.igracemusic.com/hymns/come-thou-fount-of-every-blessing. Accessed November 4, 2020.

Chapter 5: The Fortitude of Courage

1. Brené Brown, October 3, 2012. "Vulnerable, Brave and Awake." Podcast audio. *Good Life Project*, https://www.goodlifeproject.com /podcast/brenebrownbestof/. Accessed September 10, 2020.

2. "Courage," *Online Etymology Dictionary*, https://www.etymonline .com/word/courage. Accessed September 12, 2020.

3. Frank Baker, "The Origins, Character, and Influence of John Wesley's 'Thoughts Upon Slavery,'" *The United Methodist Church: Archives and History*, January 1, 1984. 79-81, http://archives.gcah.or g/handle/10516/5244. Accessed September 14, 2020.

4. Baker, 84.

5. Baker, 84.

6. Brian D. Lawrence, "The relationship between the Methodist church, slavery and politics, 1784-1844," Rowan University: Rowan Digital Works, Theses and Dissertations, last modified date May 24, 2018, https://rdw.rowan.edu/cgi/viewcontent.cgi?article=3573&context =etd. Accessed September 16, 2020.

7. "The Great Bull Run," The Running of the Bulls, https://www .runningofthebulls.com/about/the-great-bull-run/. Accessed September 16, 2020.

8. Winston Churchill's Speech – "Their Finest Hour" (June 18, 1940), https://winstonchurchill.org/resources/speeches/1940-the-finest-hour /their-finest-hour/. Accessed November 6, 2020.

Chapter 6: The Love of Courage

1. Philip Yancey, *Reaching for the Invisible God: What Can We Expect to Find* (Grand Rapids: Zondervan, 2000), 165.

ACKNOWLEDGMENTS

I am grateful to my wife, Karen, for her support and encouragement as I considered and wrote this book on courage. To my colleagues at Floris UMC who questioned the wisdom of trying to write a book during a global pandemic, let me say in print that you were right. I am grateful for the many ways you supported this project. Thanks to Charlie Kendall for his unflagging support of the book and the videos that accompany it. You are a great friend. Susan Salley at Abingdon offered encouragement as she opened the door to this work.

Special thanks to editor Maria Mayo, who worked tirelessly with the author. All a writer wants an editor to do is read the chapter they have created, declare that it is the most beautiful baby they have ever seen, and pronounce the work complete with a simple word of appreciation. Fortunately, Maria is not this editor. The book is richer for her insights, requests for additional effort and the guidance she offered. She exhibited courage and candor throughout the writing process, which was mingled with compassion and courtesy, even as she told me that I need not use chapter titles that all begin with "c."